Jazz Soloing Basics for Guitar

I0178623

by Barrett Tagliarino

To See Example Videos or Download Audio

monsterguitars.com/jsb

The password is bebop

About the Author

Barrett Tagliarino is a Los Angeles-based guitarist with over thirty-five years of recording, performing, and teaching experience. He's been an instructor at Musicians Institute in Hollywood since 1987, teaching lead and rhythm guitar styles, ear training, theory, and reading. Barrett contributes to magazines such as *Guitar Player* and *Guitar One*, various Hal Leonard instructional DVDs and online lessons, and is the author of over a dozen music books, including:

Chord-Tone Soloing
Rhythmic Lead Guitar
Guitar Fretboard Workbook—also available in Spanish, French, and German
Guitar Reading Workbook
Interval Studies and Lead Guitar Technique
Harmonic Minor, Melodic Minor, and Diminished Scales for Guitar
Music Theory: A Practical Guide for All Musicians

Besides recording and performing with local artists, Barrett has two instrumental CDs of his own: *Throttle Twister* (2009) and *Moe's Art* (1998), showcasing his playing and compositions in a blend of rock, blues, country, and other styles. To hear these and his latest recordings and videos, please visit his website, monsterguitars.com.

ISBN-13
978-0-9802353-6-4

ISBN-10
0-9802353-6-7

Copyright © 2019 Behemoth Publishers
All rights reserved.

Except as permitted under the United States Copyright Act of 1976, as amended, no part of this publication may be reproduced or distributed in any form without prior written permission of the publisher.

Contents

Introduction   4

1. Descending Scales   6

2. Arpeggios   12

3. Diatonic Harmony   15

4. Arpeggio Exercises   18

5. Scales on Major ii-V-Is   24

6. Minor Scales and Harmony   32

7. Harmonic Minor   37

8. Key Changes   40

9. Major Scale Modes   47

10. Motifs, Quotes, and Blues Licks   53

11. Lines on Longer Chords   58

12. Arpeggios in Major-Key Lines   66

13. Long ii-V-Is   71

14. Jazz Blues   77

15. Altered Dominants   83

16. Rhythm Changes   88

17. Form And Pacing   96

Appendix 1: The Fretboard   101

Appendix 2: Interval Theory   105

Appendix 3: Notation and Key Signatures   109

Appendix 4: Playing Intervals   112

Appendix 5: Chords are Stacks of Intervals   117

Introduction

This book explains how you can train yourself to compose and improvise solos over standard jazz chord progressions, with a sense of movement and swing. If you've tried using the usual major and minor scales but they don't seem to sound like they fit, you're in the right place. We'll take our time getting there, but by about Chapter 13 you'll know how to spell out the changes so well you don't actually need anyone playing chords behind you.

Rather than just memorize sample solos and long licks, expecting them to soak in and come back out as fresh statements over other songs, we're going to learn how to construct working improvised lines on the fly, one note at a time and very slowly at first, then build up the tempo with time and practice.

This means a larger investment in time and effort at the beginning but a bigger payoff in the end. To keep your level of motivation up, I recommend moving through the book at a steady pace, forging ahead to later chapters before the foundation material is completely memorized. Try to find a balance of challenge and ease in your practice regimen, and expect to occasionally run up against something that requires you to stop and review scales, chords, or arpeggios.

The most important musical goal of this book is actually rhythmic. The right note is only right when you play it at the right time. If you're not used to counting and playing at the same time, this will be a hurdle. Don't try to dodge it. Go as slowly as you must so that you can keep track of each pitch and which beat it happens on, stepping through the measure one eighth note at a time if necessary before turning on the metronome or backing track. I can't emphasize this enough.

Learning Faster

Some of my fastest-learning students over the last 35 years have been so motivated to get these sounds happening that they will plow ahead before they completely master the basics. They know they need to review but they only do it in short bursts as needed. As a result they are jumping back and forth constantly, studying many things concurrently. Traditional teaching methods might discourage such an apparently disorganized approach to learning, but double-blind studies over the last few decades have shown that the strategies of **pre-testing** and **interleaving** are more efficient for acquiring new skills and information. Topics in this book will be presented in isolation when possible for easier comprehension and initial practice but should be practiced all together in an interleaved fashion as soon as possible.

An important part of self-teaching is finding ways to stay motivated and focused. If you are working alone in a vacuum it's going to be hard. Study music you're intrigued and challenged by as much as possible and try to find an outlet for performing it.

Even the most disciplined among us do better when we have externally-imposed structure and deadlines. These can be created by signing up for classes or lessons, and seeking out and taking gigs that we know will challenge us. Join a band or go to a jam even if you're not sure you can nail it yet. Ten minutes of sweating on stage is worth hours of practice in the safety of your room. If you can't find any place to play out in public where you live, at least commit to recording and posting your playing online regularly.

The more abstract and challenging something is, the more important to work on it in little pieces. With that in mind, you'll be getting small but essential bits of music theory as needed along the way. Pay close attention to these if they are new to you.

You should be familiar with major and minor scales all over the neck. We'll review them before using them and will go back to them again and again. It's OK if you use 3-note-per-string scales, but be aware that they may not directly correspond to the chord shapes as do the scales in the CAGED-based 5-pattern system.

Here's a more complete list of things it would be good to know about before you start.
• CAGED-based 5 pattern fretboard system (Appendix 1)
• Names of notes on the fretboard
• Chord and scale diagrams
• Tablature
• Rudimentary music notation (eighth notes and triplets, key signatures and accidentals. Appendix 3)
• Triads and 7th Chords in at least two positions on the fretboard (Appendix 5)
• Half steps and whole steps, intervals from unison to 13th (Appendices 1, 2)
• Naming conventions for chords (Chapters 2, 3, 5; Appendix 5)
• Circle of Fourths/Fifths

You need a good practice space where you can leave everything set up and ready to go: a playback system for rhythm tracks, a metronome, book on the music stand with some clips to hold it in place, guitar out of the case. At least one book of jazz standards like *The Real Book, 6th Edition, for C Instruments* is essential. That one in particular has permission to reprint its copyrighted songs. Publishers can and usually do prohibit printing of their music (unlike the compulsory license for sound recordings), so no tunes are shown in this book beyond short quotes within solos.

Here are some of the tunes that are referenced in this book. Memorize the chords and melodies or be at least somewhat familiar with as many as you can. Most are in the 6th Edition Real Book (which is really a *fakebook*).

Autumn Leaves
Blue Bossa
Tune Up
Softly, As In A Morning Sunrise
Solar
Little Sunflower
Cantaloupe Island
Mr. P.C.
Stolen Moments
Equinox
Footprints
Oleo
I Love You
Just Friends
Love For Sale
Willow Weep For Me
Au Privave
The Days Of Wine and Roses
Blues In The Closet
Sandu
Here's That Rainy Day

Chapter 1: Descending Scales

▶ jsb01

This set shows all five major scale patterns of the CAGED system. The patterns let you play all over the neck in any key. Pattern 1 is a D major scale if your **pinky** (4th) finger plays the circled "1" on fret 5 of string 5 (the A string). Moving up (toward the body) to play the same note (fret 5, string 5) with your **middle** finger puts you in position for Pattern 2 of D major, which shares a "1" with Pattern 3 on string 3, etc. If this is unclear, check out Appendix 1, pp. 101-105.

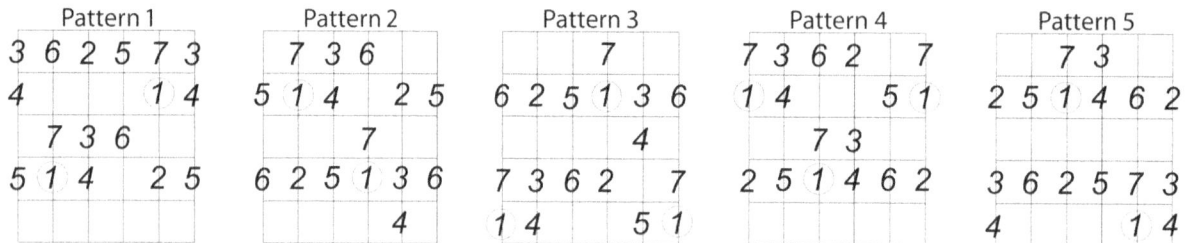

Pattern 1	Pattern 2	Pattern 3	Pattern 4	Pattern 5
3 6 2 5 7 3	7 3 6	7	7 3 6 2 7	7 3
4 1 4	5 1 4 2 5	6 2 5 1 3 6	1 4 5 1	2 5 1 4 6 2
7 3 6	7	4	7 3	3 6 2 5 7 3
5 (1) 4 2 5	6 2 5 1 3 6	7 3 6 2 7	2 5 1 4 6 2	4 1 4
	4	1 4 5 1		

Three Basic Jazz Rhythm Feels for Soloing

Within the following basic categories there are many variations of tempo, accent patterns, and note durations, but for most of this book we'll be trying to master the swung eighth note in 4/4 time.

4/4 Swing

We'll practice the above scales in eighth notes (two notes for each foot tap) with a *swing* feel. This means that the notes on the beat (1, 2, 3, 4) are slightly longer than the ones on the "ands," making them start a little later, creating a little bounce. It's similar to a blues shuffle like "Green Onions," only more subtle. If your feel is a little too bouncy at first, that's ok. Continued practice in this rhythm will refine it over time.

3/4 Swing (also called *Jazz Waltz*)

Although the individual notes feel the same as they do in 4/4 swing, soloing over this groove will be hard at first, because we're accustomed to hearing the downbeat in a different place. When we practice scales on the next page, it'll just so happen that one guitar position randomly lends itself to 3/4, so we'll hear that soon. Check out "Someday My Prince Will Come" for a familiar example. Miles Davis did a good version.

The faster the metronome is set, the closer swing eighth notes will feel to straight ones. At a high enough tempo (e.g. 180 bpm or higher) they will sound the same. This usually happens naturally and you don't need to worry about it now.

4/4 Straight Eighth-Note

When you play a scale in straight eighth notes along with a metronome, the note attacks are evenly spaced, two per beat. These feel the same for soloing purposes for rock grooves, most Latin grooves like bossa novas and rumbas, and straight eighth-note jazz-rock tunes like "Cantaloupe Island."

We don't want starting low to always be the first thing we do by reflex when it's time to improvise. To start practicing scales, let's descend from the high root (the "1"), play all the available notes in the pattern, and return to the high root.

Key changes are an important part of jazz tunes, so we need to get used to finding new scales without shifting position. Here we'll follow the most common key change, moving up by a perfect 4th interval each time.

This means that after playing a pattern, you'll go to its 4th degree and start a new scale. After C major Pattern 3 (with roots on strings 6, 3, and 1) you will play F major Pattern 1, with roots on strings 5 and 2. Move to step 4 of F, and start again, now in B♭, and so on.

To prepare your scale knowledge for future use, recite the degree numbers in the above pattern diagrams aloud as you play. You'll eventually know how to quickly find or identify any degree of a scale so you can relate it to chords, arpeggios, melodies, licks, and other scales.

C Major Pattern 3

F Major Pattern 1

B♭ Major Pattern 4

E♭ Major Pattern 2

A♭ Major Pattern 5

```
T ---9-8-6-------------------------------------------6-8--9-8-6----------
A --------8-6-5---------------------5-6-8--5-6-8---6-8-9-----------9------
B -------------8-6--5----------5-6-8--------------------------------------
            9-8-6-8-9   6-8
```

D♭ Major Pattern 3

```
T ---9-8-6-------------------------------------------------6-8--9--------
A --------9-7-6---------------5---------------5-6-8--6-7-9------------------
B -------------8-6--5--8-6--------6-8-9---6-8------------------------------
            9-8-6   9-8  6-8-9
```

If you continue beyond what's written above (to G♭, then B, and so on), you will cycle through all twelve keys, repeating the five fingering patterns as you move up the neck. Practice a little each day until you can do this without looking at any diagrams.

Start Anywhere

We need to be able to start from any pitch in a scale, not just the root. These next examples start from a few different high notes in Pattern 4 of C major. Learning to jump in on any tone of a scale pattern and continuing down or up without a glitch is the long-term goal.

C Major Scale, Pattern 4, descending from the 2nd, D

Dm⁷   G⁷   C

count! 1 & 2 & 3 & 4 & 1 & 2 & 3 & 4 &

```
T ---10-8-7--------------------------------------
A ----------10-8-------------------10------------
B ----------------10-9-7--------------------------
```

First we'll start on beat 1 and resolve on the downbeat of the second measure in a two-measure phrase, to help us learn to feel that important time frame. I strongly suggest counting aloud and tapping your foot on every numbered beat while you are playing **and** while you are resting or sustaining a long tone.

C Major Scale, Pattern 4, descending from the 4th, F

Dm⁷   G⁷   Cmaj⁷

```
T ---10-9-7-------------------------------
A ----------10-9-7------------------------
B ----------------10-8--7-----------------
```

The count is not shown for all; please continue counting the beats and the "ands" in between. It's an extra effort now, but it will pay off later. For Pattern 4 of C major you can stay strictly in 7th position, using one finger per fret. That means these two examples should start with the 4th finger.

Count the full two measures before starting another example or repetition. Don't let your foot stop, and don't skip the bars of sustain or rest. They're important.

C Major Scale, Pattern 4, descending from the 6th, A

Dm⁷   G⁷   Cmaj⁷

```
T  10  8
A       10  9  7
B            10  9  7
                  10
```

Even when you practice over rhythm tracks that help you keep your place, make sure you can tap your foot and count aloud.

C Major Scale, Pattern 4, descending from the root, C

Dm⁷   G⁷   Cmaj⁷

```
T  8  7
A     10  8
B        10  9  7
               10   9
```

If you try to speed up your practice by leaving beats out between repetitions, you'll just build a bad habit that'll make you lose your place when soloing.

Start Any Time

In jazz it's going to be important to keep track of which beat you are on, and especially to feel how long you have until the next downbeat.

F Major Scale, Pattern 2, from the "and" of 1

C   C⁷/E   F

1 & 2 & 3 & 4 &   1 & 2 & 3 & 4 &

```
T
A     10  9  7
B         10  8  7
               10   8
```

We need to be able to start and end lines on any down or upbeat. If counting aloud while playing eighth-note examples like these gives you any trouble at all, you can practice just counting bars and beats along with recorded music, away from your guitar, a little every day.

from beat 2

Dm⁷   C⁷   B♭

1 & 2 & 3 & 4 &   1 & 2 & 3 & 4 &

```
T
A     10  9  7
B         10  8  7
               10   8
```

On the video I'll play some typical chords under these scale practice examples to let you hear how the scale might fit. For now we have two beats per chord because it fits with a one-octave scale.

from the "and" of 2

Gm⁷   C⁷   Fmaj⁷

1 & 2 & 3 & 4 &   1 & 2 & 3 & 4 &

It's the same fingering every time here, so there's no need for tablature. I don't like tablature anyway!

from beat 3

F   Dm⁷♭⁵   Em⁷♭⁵   D♭maj⁷♭⁵

1 & 2 & 3 & 4 &   1 & 2 & 3 & 4 &

If you're not counting and playing these examples in time, they will feel like you're just playing the same thing over and over. If you **are** counting, each one will have its own rhythmic identity and feel that relates to the chords as they move by.

from the "and" of 3

Bm⁷♭⁵   E⁷   Am⁷   Dm⁷

1 & 2 & 3 & 4 &   1 & 2 & 3 & 4 &

As we progress we'll see how starting a scale just one eighth note earlier or later can either fit or clash with a chord progression, making a line either move forward or stall.

from beat 4

Em⁷♭⁵   A⁷   Dm⁷   G⁷

1 & 2 & 3 & 4 &   1 & 2 & 3 & 4 &

The correct timing of pitches will be tied to chords, either by adhering to the chords that are there, or by implying a chord move in your line.

from the "and" of 4

Bdim⁷   F/C   C♯dim⁷   Dm⁷

1 & 2 & 3 & 4 &   1 & 2 & 3 & 4 &

Any Time, Anywhere

G Major Scale, Pattern 1, from the 5th, D, on the "and" of 1

Am⁷   D⁷   Gmaj⁷

1 & 2 & 3 & 4 &   1 & 2 & 3 & 4 &

```
T  10  8  7
A        10  8  7
B              9      7
```

Finally we have scales from every 8th-note starting time and from various pitches.

```
Pattern 1
3  6  2  5  7  3
4           1  4
   7  3  6
5  1  4     2  5
```

G Major Scale, Pattern 1, from the 2nd, A, on beat 2

Am⁷   D⁷   Gmaj⁷

1 & 2 & 3 & 4 &   1 & 2 & 3 & 4 &

Again, because each of these uses the same scale pattern, I'm removing the tablature. With practice you will learn the note names and scale degrees and internalize the patterns so you can focus on the timing.

G Major Scale, Pattern 1, from the 5th, D, on the "and" of 2

Pattern 1

G Major Scale, Pattern 1, from the 3rd, B, on beat 3

Notes played before beat 1 (the *downbeat*) are called *pickup* notes. As in the other examples, you have to start counting in advance in order to come in at the right time.

G Major Scale, Pattern 1, from the 4th, C, on the "and" of 3

You don't have to worry about **why** I picked a particular starting pitch for each beat just yet. The decision will involve arpeggios, which are covered in the next chapter. For now you should just get used to finding numbered scale degrees within the pattern.

G Major Scale, Pattern 1, from the 6th, E, on beat 4

G Major Scale, Pattern 1, from the 7th, F♯, on the "and" of 4

Practice Assignment

Work out the examples on pp. 8-11 in the next higher scale pattern up the neck. Play the C major examples in Pattern 5, the F major examples in Pattern 3, and the G major examples in Pattern 2 (The penultimate one won't work in that position but you could move it down to Pattern 5 instead for practice).

Chapter 2: Arpeggios

An *arpeggio* is the notes of a chord played one at a time.

Arpeggios present new fingering challenges. Generally speaking you'll need to use **all four** fingers, with a bit of independent control that will take practice. Make sure you can cleanly arch or flatten your fingertips as needed, to get just one note to ring at a time, with little or no gap between notes, for each arpeggio pattern. Connecting the arpeggios to scale passages, moving between fretboard positions, and starting these patterns with different available fingers will add further complications.

As mentioned in the introduction, I'll assume you're familiar with major scales. Let's start with arpeggios derived from Pattern 4 of the major scale. First review the root shape and the complete major scale. As the later diagrams imply by the lack of a marker, you can do this in any key and position. I'll go with G; 1st- and 6th-string roots on fret 3.

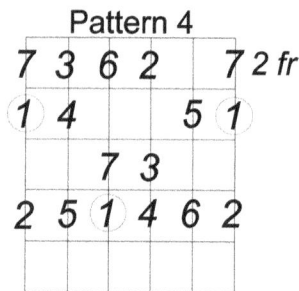

Pattern 4

```
7  3  6  2  |  7  2 fr
(1) 4       |  5 (1)
         7  3
2  5 (1) 4  6  2
```

As with scales, you want to practice each arpeggio how you'll use it most when improvising, which is a four-note subset of a full six-string shape you might have studied before. Soon we'll use these small shapes on top of different chords (for example, you might play the Gmaj7 arpeggio over an A7 chord).

Gmaj7: 1 3 5 7

Pattern 4

```
         7
      5
   3
1
```

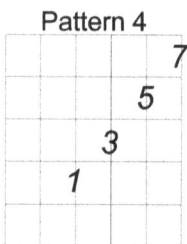

To get the Pattern 4 Gmaj7 arpeggio, play only the root, 3rd, 5th, and 7th. Make sure to only play one note at a time: arpeggio tones should not sound together as a chord. Remember, the G root ("1") is on **fret 5**. The position marker is gone because we're going to move these around for other keys. For this shape, use all four fingers.

G7: 1 3 5 ♭7

Pattern 4

```
      5
   3
1
   7
```

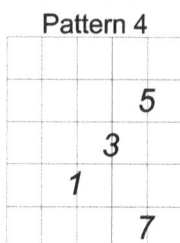

To make it a G7 arpeggio, flat the 7th by a half step. (Instead of the verb "diminish," "flat" is used as a shorthand.) All other pitches stay the same, although now you should start with the ring finger instead of the pinky. To keep within a reachable span the 7th (F) is played on string 2.

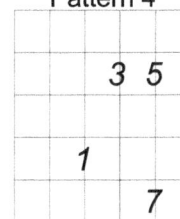

Along with the 7th, now flat the 3rd to get Gm7. The root's still on fret 5.

Gm7: 1 ♭3 5 ♭7

Pattern 4

	3	5
1		
	7	

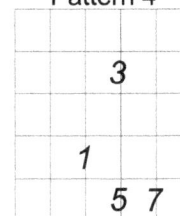

Continuing, flat the 5th now, to get the Gm7♭5 arpeggio. It's a little dissonant but this arpeggio and the m7♭5 chord are used quite often. This quality is also called "half-diminished" in some areas.

G∅7: 1 ♭3 ♭5 ♭7

Pattern 4

	3	
1		
5	7	

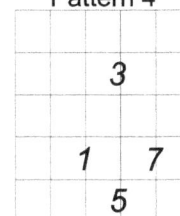

Finally, by flatting the 7th again, we get the "fully diminished" Gdim7 arpeggio. Its diminished 7th is *enharmonic* (the same pitch spelled differently) with the major 6th, E.

G°7: 1 ♭3 ♭5 ♭♭7

Pattern 4

	3	
1	7	
5		

We just compared various qualities from the same root. You'd be hard-pressed to find a song with chords that actually follow this order, so there's no need to get this particular series of arpeggios up to speed. You only need to get the shapes and sounds into your head, and comparing them side by side is a good way to understand them.

In upcoming chapters we'll add arpeggio patterns to cover the entire fretboard on all strings, keys and positions, but for now, prioritize these four-note shapes. On the next page are five patterns of the five qualities. Go across the rows (moving up the neck), and also down the columns (staying in position). Play them all with D as the "1" at first, then try changing keys by fourths as we did with scales. It'll be useful to include the higher four-note arpeggio available on the top of Pattern 2 that looks like an alternate fingering for Pattern 3.

The best way to learn these is to slowly and accurately play each arpeggio just once or twice at least once per day for a couple months. Make this just a few minutes on your overall practice list. Try to pull the shapes out of your brain and avoid looking at the diagrams again unless you really get stuck. This temporary forgetting and relearning will cement the information long-term. Don't expect to memorize them in a day. If you drill them over and over, you'll build up technique and speed, but I can't say you'll learn to find or apply them any faster. You **can** do that by interleaving them with other information; for example, by using them over progressions as soon as possible.

maj7

Pattern 1
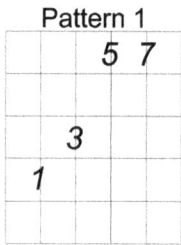

Pattern 2
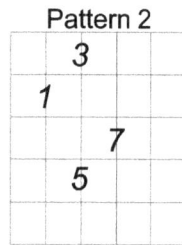

Pattern 3
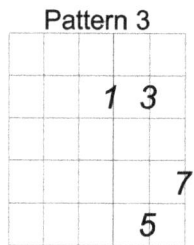

Pattern 4
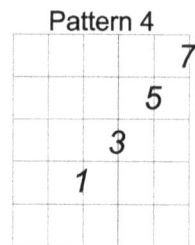

Pattern 5
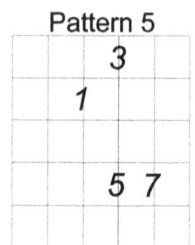

dominant 7

Pattern 1
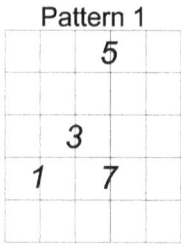

Pattern 2
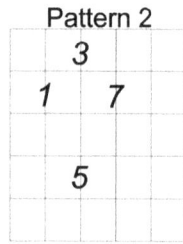

Pattern 3
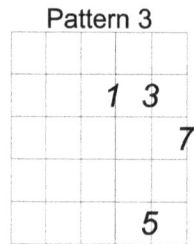

Pattern 4
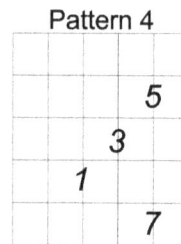

Pattern 5
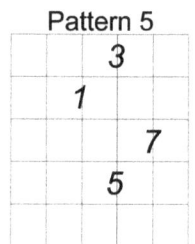

minor 7

Pattern 1
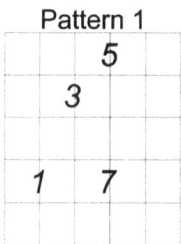

Pattern 2
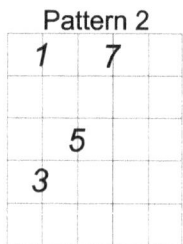

Pattern 3
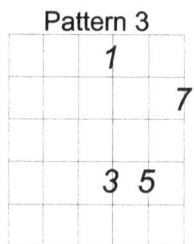

Pattern 4
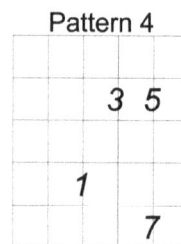

Pattern 5
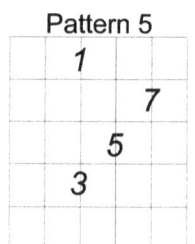

m7♭5

Pattern 1
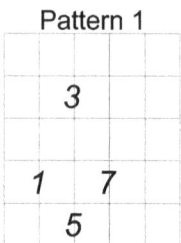

Pattern 2
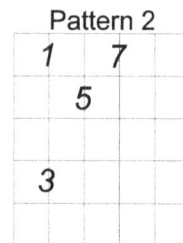

Pattern 3
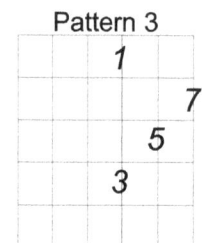

Pattern 4
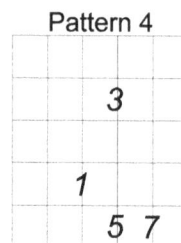

Pattern 5
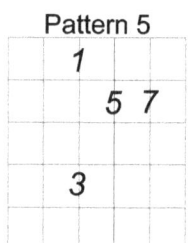

dim7

Pattern 1
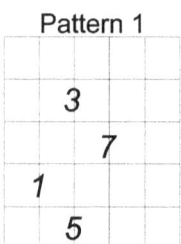

Pattern 2
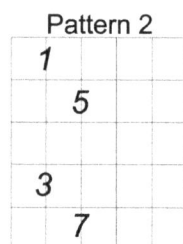

Pattern 3
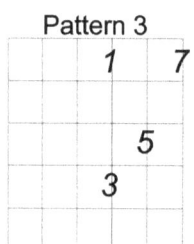

Pattern 4
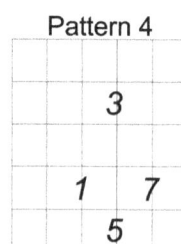

Pattern 5
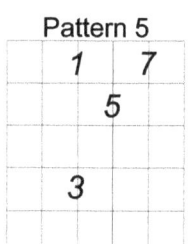

Chapter 3: Diatonic Harmony

The word *diatonic* comes from the Greek roots *dia* (**across** or **through**, as in *diagonal* or *dialog*) and *tonos* (tone). In the musical realm *diatonic* refers to anything that is restricted to a single scale (a span of tones). We have diatonic intervals, melodies, arpeggios, and chords: those that only contain notes from within one scale.

We know about key signatures as they relate to scales, but let's define a *key* as the sensation that one pitch (the root or *tonic*) is central to a song or section. It's the one note we hear as the most obvious to play when a song ends. The key also includes a *tonality*: major or minor, created primarily by the 3rd degree of the scale. The key tells us which major or minor scale a melody is based on, and in turn that scale is also the source of most of the chords.

For any major key there are seven basic diatonic chords. The chords are built using alternating notes of the major scale. They're the same maj7, min7, dom7, and m7♭5 chords we've arpeggiated, now placed in order from I-vii in the key of C.

Thirteen scale steps are written, because we'll need to go that high to get all the notes in the last chord, Bm7♭5. The half steps of the scale from 3-4 and 7-8 (and 10-11) are marked with angular carets above. The notes of the "one" or Imaj7 chord are marked below: the 1st, 3rd, 5th, and 7th notes of the scale: C–E–G–B. The *close voicing* of the Imaj7 chord (the simplest way to see it), is added at the end of the line.

The diatonic iim7 ("two") chord in the key of C uses steps 2, 4, 6, and 8 of the scale. Because there is a half step from 3-4 in the major scale (E to F in this key), this chord starts with a minor 3rd, then has a perfect 5th and minor 7th.

The iii chord uses steps 3, 5, 7, and 9. In the key of C that's an Em7 chord.

Carrying on with this process we get the seven diatonic chords, with these qualities, in this order: major-minor-minor-major-dominant-minor-minor7♭5 (It's a thing to memorize.)

The chords will be easier to play on the guitar if we rearrange the notes, in this case raising the 3rd by an octave. (Sometimes these are called *drop voicings*, a topic best left for a rhythm guitar book.) Try playing these chords up the neck. This is a **harmonized major scale**. Finish this series with a Cmaj7 chord at the 15th fret just like the one at the 3rd fret. Then play the chords in reverse order, returning to Cmaj7 at fret 3.

Cmaj⁷	Dm⁷	Em⁷	Fmaj⁷	G⁷	Am⁷	Bm⁷♭5

C: Imaj7   iim7   iiim7   IVmaj7   V7   vim7   viim7♭5

When this exercise is performed in other keys, we get the same chord types in the same order, but because of the guitar's tuning and physical limitations the shapes may be different. Here are the diatonic chords in the key of G, starting low on the 6th-string roots, but moving to 5th-string roots to avoid crowding the fingers. Play these up to a Gmaj7 at fret 10 (I think you can find it) and back as well.

Gmaj⁷	Am⁷	Bm⁷	Cmaj⁷	D⁷	Em⁷	F♯m⁷♭5

G: Imaj7   iim7   iiim7   IVmaj7   V7   vim7   viim7♭5

Chord Families

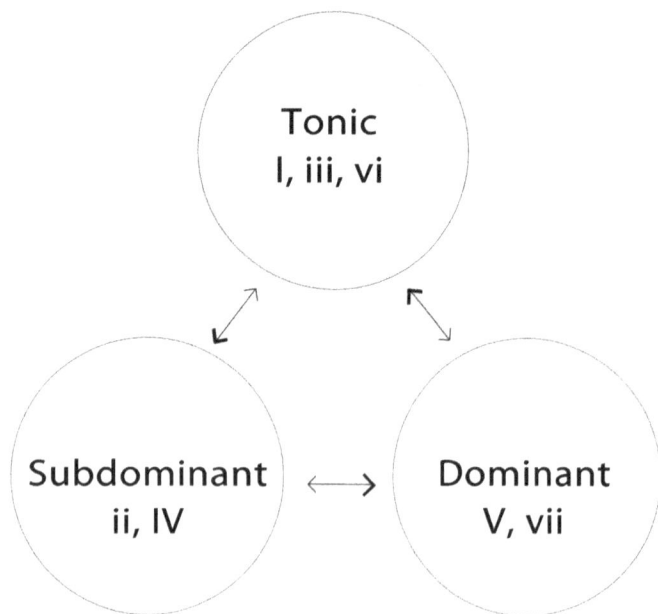

The diatonic chords in a key are divided into three families: tonic (I, iii, vi), dominant (V, vii), and subdominant (ii, IV). In minor keys the VI chord will be in the subdominant family.

Sensations of movement, tension, and resolution are created most strongly when chords progress from one family to another. The feelings described below are more like expectations, which may be strong or subtle. Of course expectations in music are not always fulfilled; we just need to recognize them.

If you're on a tonic family chord, you're starting from or have arrived at a place of stability. You can stay where you are, or easily go to a chord in either of the other two families.

Tonic
I, iii, vi

Subdominant
ii, IV

Dominant
V, vii

If you are on a dominant family chord, you may hear the tendency (tension) toward the tonic, but it's also possible to go to the subdominant.

When on a subdominant, it feels like you will move at some point, to either of the other two places.

A short chord movement that's enough to create a sense of key is called a *cadence*. It comes from the Latin *cadere*, to fall.

The strongest feelings of resolution are brought about by half-step movements within the chords. The heaviest, from V to I, is the **authentic** cadence, where the 3rd and 7th of the V chord resolve by half step to root and 3rd of the I chord.

In a **plagal** cadence, IV to I, the root of IV resolves down by a half step to the 3rd of the I. Amen, sisters and brothers.

Notice how these effects are easiest to hear when the I and IV chords are just triads (three-note chords). In many simple songs all the chords are triads or only the V chord has the 7th added.

In jazz we'll have four-note and larger chords adding sophistication and subtlety, with altered chords creating or intensifying tension-resolution effects, like the D7♭9 to Gmaj7 move. Notice that the 3rd of D7 is the same as the 7th of Gmaj7.

Though it's possible to go from one diatonic chord to any other at any time (including movement within a chord family), they're usually arranged in series of cadences to create phrases of even lengths (2, 4, or 8 measures) that can be subconsciously understood and predicted by the listener. When we play melodies and lines over these phrases we'll want to be aware of, and often reinforce, these phrase lengths.

In traditional styles like folk music, phrases most often start on the I chord, then move to others before returning to the I, with few or no key changes. In jazz or other modern styles, we'll commonly have phrases that start on the subdominant (ii), move to dominant (V), and then to tonic (I): ii-V-I cadences, or just ii-V cadences: from subdominant to dominant without a complete resolution, before moving on, possibly changing keys.

As beginning jazz soloists we especially need to get used to the sound of the key center being introduced by the iim7 chord, so we can start playing the correct major scale (or something based on our awareness of it).

Chapter 4: Arpeggio Exercises

There are a lot of ways to practice arpeggios that are OK for memorizing the shapes and conquering fingering problems, but because of their repetitious nature, not all transfer well into solos.

Playing the exact arpeggios that match a progression is never theoretically wrong but can be less than optimal. All the notes are stable and resolved over their respective chords, so you'd only have the sensations of movement provided by the chords themselves. With that said, it'll be helpful to play arpeggios directly corresponding to the chords for awhile, because it helps us follow and memorize progressions. Very soon, however, we need to learn to incorporate the "arps" into our solos in less obvious ways. In other words, straight arpeggiation of chord progressions is a door we have to walk through and keep on going. First we have to understand and get them under our fingers.

Once you have some facility, try diatonic arpeggios in sequence. Visualize and play the arpeggios inside a single scale pattern when you can, but it's OK to use a position shift if it makes for easier fingering as shown in the first example here (from Pattern 4 to 5). Feel free to try other fingering options.

Next, rather than dive to the root for each chord, ascend on one and descend on the next.

In Pattern 5 of G major, the lowest available complete arpeggio is Am7.

This useful exercise moves us closer to jazz phrasing by alternating arpeggios with scale fragments; one measure per diatonic chord, throughout a single fretboard position, in this case G major pattern 4.

Here is the same exercise in Pattern 5 of G major. I'd work it out in patterns 1, 2, and 3 as well.

Connecting Game: Strict Arpeggiation

This is like weight training for solidifying your arpeggios and outlining chord changes. It's hard work but you'll see gains in just months instead of years.

- Arpeggiate the progression for a standard jazz tune in steady 8th notes.
- Always switch by going to the closest available tone of the next chord.
- Only change direction on strings 1 and 6.
- Minimize position shifts.

This example starts in D major, then changes keys to B♭ for the next chord phrase. The arpeggios are shown in D major pattern 2, and B♭ major pattern 4. Review these two scale patterns before you start.

After 8 measures, the progression starts over. Continue by finding the closest available note while moving in the same direction. If you can keep at this for three five-minute sessions per day, you will make rapid progress.

Depending on where and in which direction you start this exercise, it'll begin to repeat (after 5 times through in this case). Move to a tone of the first chord that you haven't started on yet and do it again, or, if you're ready, move up to Pattern 3 of D major and Pattern 5 of B♭ major.

Many players apply the connecting game to each tune they learn. At first you may need to work through it by writing down or drawing diagrams of the notes, then playing through very slowly. It may be so slow at first that it's not possible to use a metronome. That's OK; in fact it's an opportunity to practice counting aloud as you make sure you are playing eight 8th notes (no more, no less) for each measure, changing right on time.

Do this exercise on a set of chords every day for about two weeks before moving to a progression from another tune. For each successive assignment find one just a little different from/harder than the one before, maybe containing one new chord move or key change. Try to stay in the zone: not too hard, not too easy, adding positions and patterns and inching up the tempos as you go.

Chapter 5: Scales on Major ii-V-Is

A descending major scale can fit (and even imply the sound of) the most common chord progression in jazz: the ii-V-I. In the key of C, those chords are Dm7, G7, and Cmaj7.

C Major Scale, Pattern 4, from C

Although you're playing in the key of C, you don't hear the Cmaj7 chord until the second measure.

We need to know and be able to identify ii-V-I cadences. When you see a minor (e.g. Dm) or m7 chord, check the chords that follow. If there is a dominant 7th chord (e.g., G7) then a major (C) or maj7 chord, you likely have a ii-V-I. Double-check by counting up the major scale from the suspected "I" chord.

$$C\ D\ E\ F\ G\ A\ B$$
$$1\ 2\ 3\ 4\ 5\ 6\ 7$$

If the 2nd and 5th scale degrees (D and G here) are the same as the m7 and dom7 chord roots on the chart, you definitely have a ii-V-I. The major scale from the root of the I chord will fit all three chords.

Written Exercise

Write out ii-V-I progressions in all twelve keys. Go as fast as you can while being 100% accurate. (Hint: play and spell the complete major scale first.)

	Dm7	G7	Cmaj7				
C:	iim7	V7	Imaj7	Gb:	iim7	V7	Imaj7

	Gm7	___	Fmaj7				
F:	iim7	V7	Imaj7	B:	iim7	V7	Imaj7

	Cm7	___	___				
Bb:	iim7	V7	Imaj7	E:	iim7	V7	Imaj7

	___	___	___				
Eb:	iim7	V7	Imaj7	A:	iim7	V7	Imaj7

	___	___	___				
Ab:	iim7	V7	Imaj7	D:	iim7	V7	Imaj7

	___	___	___				
Db:	iim7	V7	Imaj7	G:	iim7	V7	Imaj7

Now use any chord voicings you may know (Appendix 5) to play the ii-V-I cadences that you just wrote out. It's possible to play ii-V-Is in every key with just six chord voicings if you know the names of the notes on strings 5 and 6.

Also try the easy (and important) *shell* voicings; these have no 5th but function the same.

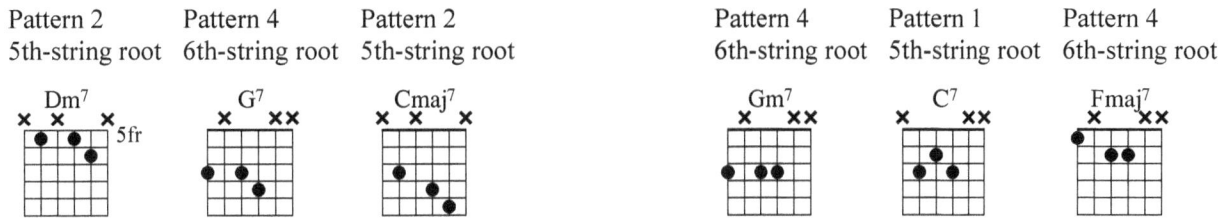

Pattern 2   Pattern 4   Pattern 2   Pattern 4   Pattern 1   Pattern 4
5th-string root 6th-string root 5th-string root   6th-string root 5th-string root 6th-string root

Dm7   G7   Cmaj7   Gm7   C7   Fmaj7

The goal is be able to find and play a ii-V-I in any key, to spot a ii-V-I (or just a ii-V) when you see it written down, and to identify one when you hear it. Sometimes a ii-V or ii-V-I cadence will only be implied or just understood to exist by players in the band, so it'll be important to know it really well.

Where to Start in the Scale

It wasn't mentioned then, but in Chapter 1's "Start Anywhere" exercise (p.8), we started the C major scale from tones of the Dm7 chord: D (its root), F (its 3rd), A (5th) and C (7th). The tones (1-m3-5-m7) of the iim7 chord are degrees 2, 4, 6, and 1 of the major scale. We need to know how notes relate to both things: the chord of the moment, and the key center.

C major scale	C	D	E	F	G	A	B	C
Scale degrees	1	2	3	4	5	6	7	1
Dm7 tones		1		m3		5		m7

These two diagrams show the two different ways to consider the tones of the Dm7 chord in the key of C at the 7th fret. Root shape 3 of D resides within Pattern 4 of C. (Please assume 3rds and 7ths are minor in diagrams labeled "m.") Although now we're only using a single tone of the iim7 chord to start a scale from, we want to think of it as part of an arpeggio.

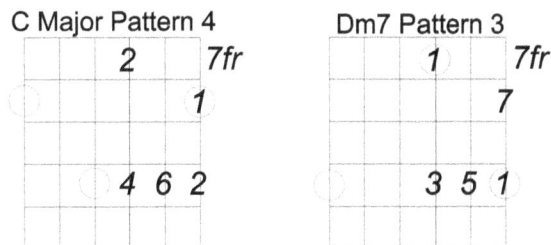

C Major Pattern 4   Dm7 Pattern 3

```
        2       7fr                  1       7fr
            1                            7

      4 6 2                          3 5 1
```

A descending major scale starting on beat 1 from **any tone of the ii chord** will fit over a **short** ii-V-I (two beats on each chord), and it will resolve onto the I chord. Go to pages 8-9 (if needed) and review the short ii-V-I lines in Cmajor. Then come back here and let's find those starting places in the key of F: the tones of its ii chord, Gm7. (Diagrams on next page.)

F major	F	G	A	B♭	C	D	E	F
Scale degrees	1	2	3	4	5	6	7	1
Gm7 tones		1		m3		5		m7

F major Pattern 2   Gm7 Pattern 1

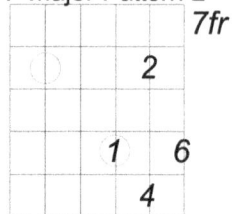

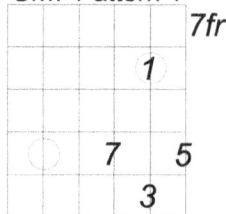

F Major Scale, Pattern 2, from the root of iim7: G

Gm⁷   C⁷   Fmaj⁷

F Major Scale, Pattern 2, from the 3rd of iim7: B♭

Gm⁷   C⁷   Fmaj⁷

Legato Technique

Scalar phrases lend themselves to the use of *slurs* on the guitar: pulloffs, hammer-ons, and slides. Pick the upbeat note and slur into the downbeat note (when it's on the same string) to get the right vibe. If you pick the downbeat notes and slur into the upbeats, it usually won't have quite the same swing feel.

F Major Scale, Pattern 2, from the 5th of iim7: D

Gm⁷   C⁷   Fmaj⁷

F Major Scale, Pattern 2, from the 7th of iim7: F

Gm⁷   C⁷   Fmaj⁷

Descending Short ii-V-I Exercise

Review each major scale of the five-pattern system in the key of D, then play only degrees 2, 4, 6, and 1 of each on the top three strings. These are all Em7 arpeggios. Practice descending scales from these notes over short ii-V-I progressions in D major. Patterns 1, 2, and 3 of the exercise are shown on the next page. Please continue through Patterns 4 and 5. Add this exercise to your practice log and play it in a different key each day for two weeks or more.

Position: II

Pattern 1

Position: IV

Pattern 2

Position: VI

Pattern 3

This example is pretty minimal, but if you get it up to a decent tempo it will feel sort of like a soulless nursery-school zombie version of jazz. Learn the composed solo, play it a few times, and make sure you understand it.

Before starting, make sure you can play the chords as written on beats 1 and 3, with solid timing. Then review Pattern 3 of the C major scale, with roots on strings 6, 1, and 3 around fifth position. The chords are all diatonic to the key of C major, so this is the only scale you'll need for now. There are two short ii-V-Is, with a partial descending line in measure 3 and an octave-long one in measure 8.

At least temporarily memorize the progression and the written solo. Get the notes off the page and try not to look at them again unless you get stuck. This will free you to listen more closely to how the solo relates to the chords. Each measure has a chord tone on beat 1. For example, the first note is G, the fifth of the Cmaj7 chord. I suggest playing this note with your 2nd finger so that the rest of the scale pattern falls into place. Identify any arpeggios as you see/hear them.

After learning the solo, if you want to, feel free to improvise using the C major scale, trying to hear how sometimes notes from the major scale can sound wrong, even though they're theoretically right, because of **when** they are played on each chord with regard to the beat. If you do improvise on the progression, use nothing smaller than an eighth note so that you train yourself to accurately track the underlying rhythm. If you want to play faster, set the tempo of the backing track as high as you like—but keep playing eighth notes.

Next up will be an improv practice routine on this progression for getting that timing control.

Jazz Study #1: Scaly Crawler

Now that we've practiced scales and arpeggios and have a chord progression to work with, we have enough to start a practice routine that can be applied to all the études in the book and every tune you want to solo over from now on. This is where the rubber meets the road.

We'll loop a section for several minutes at a time and practice hitting target notes. Here's how to take it step by step, for this or any other progression that has chord changes.

• Make a 5-minute backing track by playing the chords in time with a metronome at a slow tempo. Start around 60 bpm. Play the chords right on beat 1 or 3. You can also use an app to play the backing, but make sure you don't neglect your chord-playing practice.

• Write the letter name of a target tone for each chord on the chart. I often start my students out with just the root of each chord, especially if they're not very familiar with arpeggios and the names of the notes on the fretboard.

• Find all these target tones in a small area of the fretboard. This time I'm using 5th position, on the top four strings.

• Run the backing track and play only the notes you have written, right on the beat. That's shown here.

• When you can find the above notes consistently, find and review the scale pattern(s) that apply to the chord changes. For this progression, that's the C major scale only. Later ones will have multiple scales and possible key changes.

• Repeat the previous run through, preceding each target note with a scale tone directly above or below.

After finding and playing the roots, make another copy of the chart with different target tones. Focus on 3rds and 7ths of the chords at first; they imply chord qualities and give a sense of movement. In time you will make melodic choices that include all possible target tones, even some very dissonant ones.

This version targets the 3rd of each chord from a diatonic step above or below.

For this example I used the main notes from the original solo on the étude. Each chord is targeted on its root, 3rd, 5th, or 7th.

Here are the same target tones with one-note scale approaches added before each.

Also apply the arpeggio connecting game (p.22) to help yourself find target tones.

When you create similar exercises for yourself, set them up so that your task is challenging, yet attainable. For example, stay in one area of the fretboard on four strings until you are fairly confident leading into 3rds and 7ths by one eighth note with few mistakes. Then gradually add longer lead-ins, raise the tempo, increase the range, move to new positions, change the key, etc.

It's up to you to keep track of your own progress and administer the pace of increasing difficulty. No one else could do it for you, unless they were to monitor you at all times during your practice.

Chapter 6: Minor Scales And Harmony

The Natural Minor Scale

Pattern 1 is a D minor scale if your 4th finger plays the leftmost circled "1" on the A string at fret 5. Playing that same note with your 1st finger puts you in position for Pattern 2 of D minor, and so on.

Pattern 1
```
    2 5
4 7 3 6 1 4
       2 5 1
5 1 4 7 2 5
6       3 6
```

Pattern 2
```
5 1 4 7 2 5
6       3 6
  2 5 1
7 3 6   4 7
```

Pattern 3
```
2 5 1
7 3 6   4 7
    2
1 4 7 3 5 1
        6
```

Pattern 4
```
      2
1 4 7 3 5 1
        6
2 5 1   2
3 6     7 3
```

Pattern 5
```
2 5 1 4   2
3 6       7 3
    2 5
4 7 3 6 1 4
```

As with other scales, we want to train a slight preference for starting high and descending but be familiar with every available note within a position.

A Minor Pattern 4

D Minor Pattern 2

G Minor Pattern 5

C Minor Pattern 3

F Minor Pattern 1

B♭ Minor Pattern 4

As you continue (with E♭ minor, A♭ minor, etc.) you'll slowly move up the fretboard in a repeating series of patterns.

Start Anywhere, Any Time

Again, we need to be able to start a scale on any of its tones, from any beat. Don't worry too much about the chords I'm putting under these examples. I'm just trying to cast scales in a good light. They get a bad rap sometimes.

E Minor Scale, Pattern 2, from the 5th, B, on the "and" of 1

E Minor Scale, Pattern 2, from the 2nd, F♯, on beat 2

E Minor Scale, Pattern 2, from the 7th, D, on the "and" of 2

E Minor Scale, Pattern 2, from the 6th, C, on beat 3

E Minor Scale, Pattern 2, from the 4th, A, on the "and" of 3

Relative Minor and Major

Each minor scale is the same as a major scale started from its 6th degree. For example, F♯ minor Pattern 4 is equal to A Major Pattern 3. F♯ minor is the *relative minor* of A.

The guitarist's shortcut to change from A minor to A major is to jump three frets down and play the same shape. This works great as long as you remember not to try to resolve your licks onto F♯.

Since the relative scales share the same key signature, they also share the same diatonic chords. The vi chord of the major key is the tonic (i) in the minor key. Here are the diatonic chords in A minor compared with C major.

	Am^7	Bm^{7b5}	Cmaj^7	Dm^7	Em^7	Fmaj^7	G^7
Am:	i	ii	^{b}III	iv	v	^{b}VI	^{b}VII
C:	vi	vii	I	ii	iii	IV	V

If you need the practice, state the relative minors to the major keys. Find accurate names by writing out and counting up the major scale formula, with half steps from 3-4 and 7-8 (1 2 3^4 5 6 7^8), to find the 6th degree.

1. C   Am   C D E^F G A B^C
2. F   Dm   F G A^B^b C D E^F
3. B^b _____   B^b C D^E^b F G A^B^b
4. E^b _____
5. A^b _____
6. D^b _____
7. G^b _____
8. F$^\sharp$ _____
9. B   _____
10. E   _____
11. A   _____
12. D   _____
13. G   _____

To go the other way, name the relative majors for the minor keys. It's always up a minor 3rd.

1. Am   C
2. Em   ___
3. Bm   ___
4. F$^\sharp$m ___
5. C$^\sharp$m ___
6. G$^\sharp$m ___
7. D$^\sharp$m ___
8. E^{b}m   ___
9. B^{b}m   ___
10. Fm   ___
11. Cm   ___
12. Gm   ___
13. Dm   ___

Minor Progressions

Diatonic minor-key progressions seem to happen more in tunes that have a straight (Latin, funk, rock, etc.) rather than a swing feel. This example uses D minor Patterns 2 and 1 to facilitate some slides and pull-offs. All the chords are diatonic and you could improvise successfully using the D minor scale only. Notice how the ii-V in F at measure 8 resolves nicely to its relative.

Jazz Study #2: Minor Distraction

Improv Practice

Arpeggiate (p.22) the above progression, then apply the steps described on pp. 29-31:

- Make a 5-minute backing track by playing the chords in time with a metronome at a slow tempo. Play the chords right on beat 1 or 3.

- Write the letter name of a target tone for each chord on the chart.

- Find and play all these target tones in a small area of the fretboard, on time, over the backing track.

- Find and review the scale patterns that apply to the chord changes.

- Run through the track, preceding each target note with a scalar lead-in of one or more notes directly above or below.

- Repeat while maintaining a balance of difficulty that keeps you focused.

Chapter 7: Harmonic Minor

In many minor-key songs, the diatonic vm7 chord is changed to a dominant seventh chord. In the key of Dm for example, instead of Am7 you can have A7, increasing the tension toward the tonic chord. To follow the new chord, temporarily switch to the harmonic minor scale. It's the same as natural minor but has a raised 7th, which is the major 3rd of the dominant V7 chord. Here are harmonic minor patterns, with position marks for the key of D minor.

Pattern 1	Pattern 2	Pattern 3	Pattern 4	Pattern 5

Pattern 1 (2fr):
```
    2 5 7  2fr
4  b3 b6 1 4
7
5 1 4    2 5
b6    b3 b6
```

Pattern 2 (4fr):
```
    7           4fr
5 1 4     2 5
 b6       7 b3 b6
    2 5 1
  b3 b6   4
```

Pattern 3 (6fr):
```
b6       7    b6 6fr
   2 5 1
  b3 b6   4
7        2    7
 1 4   b3 5 1
```

Pattern 4 (9fr):
```
7        2    7 9fr
 1 4   b3 5 1
     7   b6
 2 5 1 4     2
  b3 b6      b3
```

Pattern 5 (11fr):
```
       7       11fr
2 5 1 4    2
 b3 b6       b3
       2 5 7
  4  b3 b6 1 4
```

Memorizing all these patterns can look like a big job, and it is. It does help to relate everything (including your arpeggios) back to the five patterns of major, with natural and harmonic minor being variations on those. That way at least you always know where the roots, 2nd, 4ths, and 5ths are.

Anywhere, Any Time III: The Berserker

As with other scales, we need to start harmonic minor from any degree and any beat. Since you've seen this demonstrated before, I'll save space and encourage you to work it out for this scale on your own.

The Short ii-V in Minor

With the change to the minor harmony we get the second most common jazz cadence. Most m7♭5 chords on a jazz chart start a minor ii-V or ii-V-i. As with major ii-Vs, we want to spot these on charts and also hear the m7♭5 chord as the possible beginning of a minor-key cadence. Check to see if a m7♭5 chord is followed by a dominant chord up a fourth.

$$
\begin{array}{ccccccc}
C & D & E^\flat & F & G & A^\flat & B^\flat \\
1 & \underline{2} & 3 & 4 & \underline{5} & 6 & 7
\end{array}
$$

When descending stepwise over a short minor ii-V, you can use harmonic minor over both chords if you follow the guide we learned for short major ii-Vs: start from a tone of the iim7♭5 chord on beat 1. If there's a im7 chord in the next measure as in these examples, switch back to natural minor. Harmonic minor is a scale to practice getting into and right back out of. It's a change of just one note in the minor key.

C Harmonic Minor from the root of iim7♭5: D

Dm7♭5   G7   Cm7

```
T  3
A    5  4
B       6  5  3
                6  5  3
                      6
```

C Harmonic Minor from the 3rd of iim7♭5: F

C Harmonic Minor from the 5th of iim7♭5: A♭

C Harmonic Minor from the 7th of iim7♭5: C

Switching Between Natural and Harmonic Minor

When the chords last a full measure or more, the harmonic minor scale might sound awkward over tonic or subdominant seventh chords. Play the natural minor scale of the key over the iim7♭5 chord, switch to harmonic minor for the V7 (or vii°) chord, then go right back to natural minor if there is a im7 chord.

With that in mind you will sometimes hear harmonic minor being played on the im triad in your travels (one of the examples somewhere in this book has it). You can think of the leading tone (the major 7th, B natural in the key of Cm) as implying a V chord that quickly resolves back to i.

It's usually OK to keep playing the natural minor scale over the V chord in minor. On a tune where the minor ii-V is repeated many times (e.g. "Softly, As In A Morning Sunrise") too much emphasis on the leading tone can start to lose its punch. Avoiding the area and playing in another part of the scale can be a good idea. The leading tone is already present in the bar harmony.

Here's an example in G minor with natural minor over the vm7 (Dm7) and harmonic minor over the V7 (D7) chords.

Jazz Study #3: Accompanied Minors

Improv Practice

Connect arpeggios, then do the practice steps described on p. 36 to the above chord progression, creating a backing track, and writing in target tones and approaching them from their immediate neighbors above or below within the G minor scale, using G harmonic minor over the D7. Do it again tomorrow, and every day for a week!

Chapter 8: Key Changes

Key Center Identification

Identifying key centers ensures we use the correct scales to fit a progression. In Chapter 5's étude ("Scaly Crawler") there were ii-V-Is in the key of C major in two places, and your ear probably also told you that C major was the obvious chord to end the progression. Combining the ears with a little theory will give the best results as the charts get harder.

We saw in Chapter 3 (p.15) that a major key has only one diatonic dominant chord, on degree V. When you see a dominant chord, try naming that chord as V, count down to find the I, then play its harmonized scale. If the dominant chord is on G, then we are very possibly in C major. To make sure, we have to check every chord in the progression against the C major harmonized scale. In the case of "Scaly Crawler," all the chords fit, and we can write their *functions* (the Roman numerals) below in a *harmonic analysis*.

Cmaj7		Em7		Dm7	G7	Cmaj7		
C: Imaj7		iii-7		ii-7	V7	Imaj7		

Am7		G7		Fmaj7		Dm7	G7	
vim7		V7		IVmaj7		iim7	V7	

When there are no dominant chords present, we have to work a little harder to fit the chords into a key, but the process is basically the same. Here is a new progression we'll analyze.

Dm7		E♭maj7		Cm7		B♭maj7	

Remember the qualities of diatonic chords in a major key, and the half steps.

$$\text{Imaj7} \quad \text{iim7} \quad \text{iiim7} \quad \overset{\wedge}{\text{IVmaj7}} \quad \text{V7} \quad \text{vim7} \quad \text{viim7}^{\flat}5 \quad \overset{\wedge}{(\text{Imaj})}$$

The progression starts with a m7 chord, which might be ii, iii, or vi. If it is ii, then we'd be in the key of C, right? But we know the chords from the key of C are Cmaj7-Dm7-Em7-Fmaj7-G7-Am7-Bm7♭5. These chords do not fit.

Let's try making Dm7 the iii chord. In that case, we'd count down two whole steps to find B♭ as a possible I chord. That harmonized scale is B♭maj7-Cm7-Dm7-E♭maj7-F7-Gm7-Am7♭5. The above progression matches these chords and so is probably iiim7-IVmaj7-iim7-Imaj7 in the key of B♭.

We could also do this by seeing what happens if we try one of the major chords as I or IV. The result would be the same: the progression is in B♭ major and only the B♭ major scale would work over all the chords with no change.

The same basic process applies to identifying minor keys, but with the addition of the dominant V chord to minor harmony (Chapter 7), minor keys often have either or both of two dominant chords, V7 and ♭VII7. It's quicker to look for any m7♭5 chord in the progression. These are usually part of a iim7♭5-V7.

	B♭maj7		C7		Em7♭5	A7		Dm7		
Dm:	♭VImaj7		♭VII7		iim7♭5	V7		im7		

Note that I've used the terms "very possibly," "often," and "usually" in these explanations. There can be non-diatonic chords in a progression that can make it hard to identify the key. We'll see some of those later in the book. When you encounter short-duration non-diatonic chords surrounded by chords in the same key, they don't qualify as key changes but temporary deviations that may get a special scale or just be arpeggiated. I will point out some non-diatonic chords and what scales apply to them as we go. For now it's enough to know that they can be there without causing a complete key change.

	Amaj7		F♯m7		Fmaj7		Bm7	E7		
A:	Imaj7		vim7		**♭VImaj7**		iim7	V7		

Key Changes

A key change happens when chords different from the original key establish a new tonal center in the listener's ear. This usually requires more than one measure of time.

Another term for key change is *modulation*. There are two types: *direct* and *pivot chord*. A direct modulation happens when you encounter a chord that does not belong in the old key and starts a key change.

Direct Modulation

	F♯m7	B7		Emaj7		Fm7	B♭7		E♭maj7		
E:	iim7	V7		Imaj7		E♭: iim7	V7		Imaj7		

There is no Fm7 chord in E major, and the chords that follow Fm7 point to E♭ major. Over the direct modulation you'll switch to the correct scale for the new key right as, or maybe a beat before, the new key starts.

In the pivot chord modulation, one or more chords in common transition between the old key and the new.

Pivot Chord Modulation

	Dm7	B♭		C7	Fmaj7		Am7	D7		Gmaj7		
F:	vim7	IV		V7	Imaj7		iiim7					
							G: iim7	V7		I		

Am7 is the pivot chord here, found in both F major and G major. It'll usually be better to switch scales to the new key on or right before the even phrase boundary. The distinction between the two types of modulation is made here mostly to make sure we don't miss the key change.

When preparing to solo over progressions with key changes, take note of which pitches are shared (*common tones*) between the scales. In the previous direct modulation example, the common tones between the two keys are A♭ and E♭ (G♯ and D♯ in the old key). The last chord of the old key and the first chord of the new key have an A♭ in common, so you could sustain or repeat that pitch through the transition. Note that when a tune contains lots of key changes and/or nondiatonic notes and chords, it may be written without a key signature.

F♯m⁷   B⁷   Emaj⁷   Fm⁷   B♭⁷   E♭maj⁷

From a guitarist's perspective, the half-step key change might seem easier than the next one because you can just move a fingering pattern or a complete lick down by one fret.

F♯m⁷   B⁷   Emaj⁷   Fm⁷   B♭⁷   E♭maj⁷

In the pivot chord modulation example, the common tones between keys are G, A, C, D, and E. This key change will be easier to play over when you know your scale patterns well. In order to switch smoothly it'll be best to stay in position and use, for example, Pattern 1 of F followed by Pattern 5 of G. The last chord of the old key and the first chord of the new key have A, C, and E in common.

Dm⁷   B♭maj⁷   C⁷   Fmaj⁷   Am⁷   D⁷   Gmaj⁷

It's useful to practice repeating and varying motifs or melodic fragments across the key change to help maintain a thread of continuity. Here the first scalar descent is echoed in m. 2 and 3, and the intervallic jump from m.1 is echoed and varied at the end.

Dm⁷   B♭   C⁷   Fmaj⁷   Am⁷   D⁷   Gmaj⁷

The key changes are labeled in this example. Learn it, play it a few times, and make sure you understand it.

We've got Pattern 2 and Pattern 4 chords spelling out ii-V-Is, and a ii-V in $A^\flat$ at the end. Make sure you can play the chords on time with a single strum or pluck, making it easy to hear the key change by letting them ring until it's time for the next chord. Then tackle the solo.

Review three descending major scales in 5th position: F, $B^\flat$, and $A^\flat$. You can also think of measure 8 as being ivm^7-$^\flat$VII^7 in the key of F, the *back door* cadence, and play F minor over it. The result will be the same, as F minor is the relative minor of $A^\flat$ major.

The first measure's notes are chord tones in a dotted eighth-note motif. The second note of this motif is played on the "and" of beat 2. The motif is varied just enough to develop a simple melody as it appears again in measures 3, 5, and 6.

There are quarter notes in measure 2, played right on the beat. A few more upbeat or "and" notes appear in meas. 6-8. Don't guess at the rhythms. Keep your foot tapping, and count aloud. As you might expect, starting an eighth-note early or late will throw the lines off and create a clash with the chords.

Jazz Study #4: Major Malfunction

Improv Practice

Although I've been instructing you to practice this way for each progression in the book, I want to reinforce the process for practicing improvisation originally described on p.22 and pp.29-31 to make sure you slow down and take dealing with key changes a little at a time. Often my students will quickly decide they don't need to write out target notes and practice with focus and deliberation. The difference in results is obvious.

• Arpeggiate the chord changes, slowly at first, then in time with a metronome. (p.22)

• Make a 5-minute backing track by playing the chords in time with a metronome at a slow tempo. Start around 60 bpm. Play the chords right on beat 1 or 3. You can also use an app to play the backing, but make sure you don't neglect your chord-playing practice.

• Write the letter name of a target tone for each chord on the chart. We'll start with the root of each chord to help ourselves get oriented, then quickly move on to other chord tone targets.

• Find all these target tones in a small area of the fretboard. This time I'm using 5th position, on the top four strings.

• Run the backing track and play only the notes you have written, right on the beat.

• When you can find the above notes consistently, find and review the scale patterns that apply to the chord changes. On the next version I've written in what those should be for this progression.

• Repeat the previous run through, preceding each target note with a **scale tone** directly above or below.

Scale: F major pattern 1

Scale: B♭ major pattern 4

Scale: A♭ major pattern 5

Sometimes you can change keys a beat early. For example, the last note in measure 8 above could be E natural, because you're about to be in the key of F major when you go back to the top anyway.

After finding and playing the roots, make another copy of the chart with different target tones. 3rds and 7ths as we have below imply chord qualities and give a sense of progression.

Here are the 3rd and 7th target tones with one-note scale approaches added before each.

F   Gm7   C7   Fmaj7   Gm7   Cm7   F7

Scale: F major pattern 1   Scale: B♭ major pattern 4

Target tones: A   F   E   E   F   B♭   A

5   B♭maj7   Cm7   F7   B♭maj7   B♭m7   E♭7

Scale: A♭ major pattern 5

D   E♭   E♭   D   A♭   D♭

In this version the targets are the main notes from the original solo on the étude. Each chord is targeted on its 3rd, 5th, or 7th, with a single eighth-note lead-in.

F   Gm7   C7   Fmaj7   Gm7   Cm7   F7

Scale: F major pattern 1   Scale: B♭ major pattern 4

Target tones: A   B♭   E   A   F   G   C

5   B♭maj7   Cm7   F7   B♭maj7   B♭m7   E♭7

Scale: A♭ major pattern 5

D   G   E♭   D   D♭   G

After going through these examples, run the track again and just jam on it without a specific agenda. Stay in the fretboard area you are familiar with and play what you hear.

Chapter 9: Major Scale Modes

It is normal to use one scale over a diatonic major progression because the chords are comprised only of notes from that major scale.

We might then predict that, for example, a C major scale will still fit Dm7 when it is a *static* chord, one that continues without a change. Now it can sound like D is the tonal center. When one chord sustains indefinitely, the ear will try to treat its root as the tonic of the key. Over a sustained Dm7 the pitches in C major now sound as one of its **modes**: D Dorian.

There is a mode name for when each degree of the major scale is treated as a static tonal center (although the 7th mode is a little too tense to create one; it usually sounds like it's on its way somewhere). The names are based on ancient names for locations in Anatolia and Greece. Memorize the names with their numbers in the order that goes along with diatonic harmony.

#	Name	Formula	Distinctive Tones
I	Ionian	1 2 3̂ 4 5 6 7̂ 8	All degrees major or perfect
ii	Dorian	1 2̂3 4 5 6̂7 8	m3 **maj6** m7
iii	Phrygian	1̂2 3 4 5̂6 7 8	**m2** m3 m6 m7
IV	Lydian	1 2 3 4̂5 6 7̂8	aug4
V	Mixolydian	1 2 3̂4 5 6̂7 8	maj3 **m7**
vi	Aeolian	1 2̂3 4 5̂6 7 8	m3 **m6** m7
vii	Locrian	1̂2 3 4̂5 6 7 8	m2 m3 **dim5** m6 m7

Ionian and Aeolian

The first mode, Ionian, is just the major scale from the root, played over or implying the sound of a major triad or maj7 chord. For example, on an E major chord you'd play the E major scale; and in a discussion like this you could call it E Ionian. This is a sound we know, but it can actually be kind of tricky to improvise in Ionian on a sustained major chord because of the scale's tendency to imply movement between chord families. This is one reason why the major pentatonic scale is often used in such a situation. It doesn't have tones 4 and 7, those which can create the most tension and are most easily used over the other chord families in a progression.

Aeolian, the sixth mode, is the same as the natural minor scale we already know. Mode theory expands on the relative major-minor concept to include scales starting from **all** the notes of the major scale.

We will eventually be using all seven modes (in addition to some other scales), but for now let's concentrate on understanding three crucial new ones: Dorian, Mixolydian, and Lydian. They'll be needed for upcoming chapters, so take your time with this if it is unfamiliar.

Dorian

The second mode, Dorian, is the sound you get when you play the notes of major scale from its second degree. As we played in Chapter 5, you can use the C major scale over a Dm7 chord, an F major scale over a Gm7 chord, a B♭ major scale over a Cm7 chord, and so on.

But if this minor chord doesn't kick off a major key progression toward the tonic, the tones of that related major scale should not be phrased in a way that implies that move. You may hear it as wrong or awkward if you do. For example, don't start an ascending C major scale from C on beat one of a Dm7 chord.

In Chapter 5, the scale was started from each tone of the minor chord. Now we want to make ourselves hear those tones as stable places in the scale. In other words, 2, 4, and 6 of the original scale are now heard as 1, 3, and 5 of the new sound. Our lines should be phrased so that they no longer point back to the root of the related major scale. Continually developing the ability to create expectations that certain chords are (or are not) upcoming is one of this book's main thrusts. To start we just try to target the tones of the chord of the moment at the beginning or end of a phrase.

Modes are usually first practiced and applied over one- or two-chord vamps. They shouldn't really "progress." Having too many chords can create the feeling of tension and resolution that will push you back into hearing the related major (or natural minor) key. In this example the Em7 and G/A are primarily just there to help us feel a two-bar phrase and the eight-bar section.

Jazz Study #5: Dorian

The Dorian example uses the notes of C major, but gets the D Dorian modality from 1) the chords, which never move to C, and 2) emphasis on the tones of the Dm triad (D, F, and A) at the beginnings and endings of phrases. The other tones (C, E, G, and B) complete the mode's distinctive sound, used carefully to make sure they do not imply a move toward a C major or A minor key. The 9th (E) and 6th (B) are marked by some sliding grace-note approaches.

Measure 5 contains one of the most-used licks in jazz and modern R&B. It's become standard so it must work! This lick contains an important concept that applies to extensions (9, 11, and 13, the same as 2, 4 and 6) on most chords. As we know, the 2nd, 4th, or 6th (E, G, or B) might sound wrong if placed on the downbeat within a scalar line that implies movement toward a chord. However, we do want to occasionally accent these notes to create a jazzy coloration. We just have to give them special treatment so that the richer harmony they create can be digested by the listener. In the cliché lick above, the 2nd is played on beat 1, then we return to emphasize it later in the measure, letting everyone know this note is the focus of attention.

It can be enough just to linger on the extended note; let it ring for an entire beat or longer. You can see this with the G (4th of D) at the end of measure 3. If you mistakenly hit an extension, try just letting it ring instead of jumping away from it. You may produce the effect of classical *appoggiatura*.

Dorian only differs from the natural minor scale by its major 6th degree (B natural in the above example). This is a note to use sparingly and with an ear to the chords. To get the 6th to work twice in this example I had to mess around with it a bit. If the 6th is used at the wrong time it can sound weak even though it's technically part of the scale.

The best way I've found to get Dorian under the fingers is to realize: yes, it's the same as a major scale a whole step down, but then forget that fact and think of it as the old familiar minor pentatonic box with the 2nd and 6th degrees added. That way you can keep track of where the chord tones are, and where those other colorful extensions are so you can phrase with the right tonal center in mind. Once you are making a few decent statements in one position of the mode, then it's ok to think about the related major scale pattern if it helps you move around the fretboard until you have the mode memorized in its own CAGED system root shapes.

Mixolydian

To find mode 5, Mixolydian, play a major scale down a fifth from the root of a dominant 7th chord. For example, to play A Mixolydian on an A7 chord, you'd think of A as degree 5 and count **down** the major scale formula (with its correct half steps) to find D. The notes of the D major scale produce the A Mixolydian sound when phrased the right way over the A7 chord.

$$1 \leftarrow 2 \leftarrow 3 \leftarrow 4 \leftarrow 5$$
$$D \quad E \quad F\sharp \; \hat{} \, G \quad A$$

Over my centuries of teaching I've noticed I was not the only student to get confused, start on the A and count five steps **up** the A major scale. That doesn't work. We're counting five steps **down** a major scale and we don't know that it's D major until we're done.

Rather than focus on the theoretical route, nowadays I'd just advise you to spell the new scale with its intervallic formula, and learn some new fingering patterns. Mixolydian is like major, but with a minor 7th.

$$A \quad B \quad C\sharp \, D \quad \hat{E} \quad F\sharp \; \hat{} \, G$$
$$1 \quad 2 \quad 3 \quad 4 \quad 5 \quad 6 \quad m7$$

Of course with time you'll notice that your new A Mixolydian Pattern 4 looks exactly like D major Pattern 2. As with Dorian, however, there are notes within Mixolydian that get different rhythmic placement or sustain from others. This example uses Pattern 4 of A Mixolydian, which is the same as Pattern 2 of D major. But I don't think it sounds like it's in the key of D.

Notice where non-chord tones get some kind of special attention like a sustain, slur, or reinforcing melodic pattern.

Jazz Study #6: Mixolydian

Lydian

When the IVmaj7 chord appears in a major-key progression, playing the related major scale automatically produces the Lydian mode. You can play Lydian by raising the 4th degree of a major scale. You'll notice it is equal to a major scale a perfect fourth lower.

Besides its natural appearance on the IV chord in major keys, the Lydian mode is also used for **any non-diatonic** major 7th chord in a progression, as well as sometimes being used instead of Ionian over the I chord for variety.

A static Lydian vamp can be just a maj7 chord, or you can add another chord that includes the 2nd, #4th, and 6th of the scale, like a major triad a whole step higher as in this example. As with other modes, the sensation is strongest when there are not too many chords pulling your ear into a different tonality.

C Lydian has the same notes as G major, but don't phrase into the G pitch as if it were the tonic. The #4 (F#) is exaggerated here to play up the difference between Lydian and Ionian.

Jazz Study #7: Lydian

Can I Use Modes on Diatonic Progressions?

This question comes up in private lessons. Switching between the various modes over a diatonic major progression (like the ii-V-Is we've studied) is not necessary as it results in the same set of notes being used. It can make your solo sound choppy and disconnected. You only need to think about one major scale over all the chords while targeting their tones (admittedly I will soon completely contradict myself about this). For example, over this progression using only chords in the key of C, playing the C major scale over all of it would automatically give you:

D Dorian on Dm7
G Mixolydian on G7
E Phrygian on Em7
A Aeolian on Am7
C Ionian on Cmaj7
F Lydian on Fmaj7

Dm7	G7	Em7	Am7	
ii	V	iii	vi	

Dm7	G7	Cmaj7	Fmaj7	‖
ii	V	I	IV	

You still want to be able to hit chord tones within the scale, and know which non-chord tones are good and which can sound like mistakes depending on how and when you play them. Awareness of modes will help develop this, but try to picture a single fingering pattern and hear the progression as one key center.

The same applies to minor progressions, except that instead of the diatonic vm7 we often have the dominant V7, allowing the switch to the harmonic minor scale for that chord. This happens so much it's almost considered to be diatonic.

A Aeolian would work over all the chords in the next example; it's an option but not completely necessary to switch to A harmonic minor for E7. You'd get these modes:

A Aeolian on Am7
C Ionian on Cmaj7
B Locrian on Bm7♭5
E Phrygian on E7 (or Em7)
D Dorian on Dm7
F Lydian on Fmaj7
G Mixolydian on G7

| Am7 | Cmaj7 | Bm7♭5 | E7 | |
| i | ♭III | ii | V | |

| Dm7 | Fmaj7 | Em7 | G7 | ‖ |
| iv | ♭VI | v | ♭VII | |

Placing the Cmaj7 chord in measure 2, rather than at the start or end of the 4-bar phrase, helps keep the progression in A minor instead of C, but real songs switch between minor and relative major all the time. When a minor-key song has a few chords that sound like they're in the relative major key it's fine to follow that tendency with your solo. However (and I've already said this, but it's worth repeating), thinking in A minor over a C major progression can sound awkward, especially if you hammer out an A minor lick that ends on A over the Cmaj7 chord.

Improv Practice

Practice soloing using the prescribed modes over the Dorian, Mixolydian, and Lydian vamps in this chapter. Then do the same for the two diatonic progressions just covered: connect arpeggios through the chord changes (p.22), then write out target tones and play them with short lead-in lines (p.36), trying to find the level of difficulty required to stay engaged and improving your chops without zoning out (if it's too easy) or getting frustrated (if it's too hard).

Chapter 10: Motifs, Quotes, and Blues Licks

▶ jsb10

Let's take a break from scales and arpeggios. Jazz solos also have lots of motific development, quoted material, and licks that share their roots with the blues.

A *motif* is the smallest musical unit the listener can identify and remember. It's usually based around a tone of the chord of the moment. A motif can be as simple as one pitch played with a strong rhythmic sense. An initial motif usually should not be complex or spectacular. The first place to grab a motif is from the original melody, possibly varied in some small way, so it's good to make sure you really know the tune over whose chords you're playing.

Below we have a single motif with multiple ways it can be repeated and varied to create a longer statement. To make the demonstration simple, the first five are all over a static B♭maj7 chord.

A. Play the same motif but start on a different spot in the measure. Here the motif starts on beat 1 in the first measure. The same motif starts on the "and" of 1 in measure 2: an eighth-note *displacement*.

B. Use the same rhythm but different pitches.

C. Play the same pitches with a different rhythm.

D. Repeat the motif but add or change notes at the end.

B♭maj7

1 & 2 & 3 & 4 & 1 & 2 & 3 & 4 &

E. Repeat the motif but change the way it starts the second time.

Motifs over Changes

B♭maj7   **E♭maj7**

Exactly repeating the same motif can sound different enough if the chords are changing. For the I-IV move in this example, no change of the motif is required because the notes on the strong beats (1 and 3) do not clash with the new chord. The F on the downbeat adds the major 9th to E♭maj7.

B♭maj7   **D♭maj7**

This time it's necessary to change a note of the motif to follow a more angular non-diatonic chord change. Note the Lydian mode on the non-diatonic ♭IIImaj7 chord.

B♭maj7   **Gm7**   **Cm7**   **F7**

If the motif is melodically simple and strong enough (and is played confidently), it can ride over the chord changes and some theoretically wrong notes may be okay. It's easier to do this when the chord moves are predictable, all in the same key, and played with restraint by a savvy accompanist. Here's motific repetition over a simple I-vi-ii-V. This is the first two bars of a progression called *rhythm changes*, which we'll be seeing again.

B♭maj7   **Dm7**   **G♭maj7**   **C♭maj7**

It's harder to make this "ignore those pesky chord changes" concept work over less-predictable chord moves. Repeating the original motif verbatim in the second measure would be a mistake here.

An Observation

The simpler the style, song form, or chord progression is, the less predictable your improvisational phrasing need be. In roots blues styles, the progressions create an obvious structure, giving you freedom to use less repetition while moving through licks to build up energy over the course of your solo. Listeners will still be able to follow the music even if not all the licks are thematically connected or supportive of the form of the chord phrases.

In a jazz setting, the progressions are more challenging for the listener to follow. All the players have more options, while all share responsibility for maintaining the thread of continuity. Randomly blowing licks over bar lines and phrase boundaries may be harder to make work in this style. Just as you have to follow key changes and correctly place tones in your lines, you need to fit and help define the chords, phrases, and sections while also staying in the groove with your nonlinear statements.

After the repetition/variation of the original motif, usually there's room in a four-bar phrase for a longer fragment that logically finishes the statement and leaves a little breathing room before the next idea. Here's a typical four-measure motif and development. Notice the statement, the variation, and the conclusion that partially echoes what came before.

More four-measure examples of this type of motific development are in the A section melodies of "Willow Weep For Me," "Au Privave," and many others. Similar phrases spread out over eight bars are in thousands of standard melodies. They're in almost every tune if you know what you're looking for.

A complicated motif can be hard to develop further. If you come up with an involved idea that you like but have difficulty hearing what should follow it, try working in the opposite direction. Make your idea the concluding phrase, then break it into smaller parts and use them as a foreshadowing buildup. Of course this means you have to work everything out in advance. That's OK as long as you can switch back to improv mode if you have trouble remembering the entire worked-out idea. Composing solos is a useful valuable practice tool.

The topics of motific development and phrasing deserved a book of their own: *Rhythmic Lead Guitar*. It has kind of a funny title, but—excuse the immodesty—it may be the book I'm most proud of. If you decide to check it out, thanks in advance, and I hope it helps you on your musical journey.

You need connection between ideas balanced with some variety. The amount of similarity vs. repetition is up to your taste, but be aware that the average listener can quickly tire of trying to make sense of a solo with many dissimilar or unconnected ideas.

Melodic Quotes

The first quote source is the "head" (main melody) of the tune. It's perfectly valid to remind the listener of the melody that goes with the chords you're now soloing over. It pays to learn the melody at more than one fretboard location, and to use bits of it as the bases for further improvisations.

Quotes can come from anywhere: other jazz standards, pop or folk melodies, TV themes, etc. It may well be that the best quotes are just hints of familiarity, not long enough to take the listener out of the moment and distract them from what follows. Although it's very common to start a phrase with a quote, they may be woven into or appended to an improvised phrase. Sometimes a quote only reveals itself on repeated listening to a recording of a favorite solo.

It's an excellent idea to start a notebook wherein you transcribe one new melody every day or two. If you can read, copping melodies from a fake book is the fastest way to start building up a repertoire. These are often rough approximations (or flat-out wrong), so also check out the original recordings. Keep at least one transcription project going whenever possible.

There's not much point in writing melodic quotes here, but some of the longer examples in this book have them, pointed out as they occur.

Blues Licks

These are another crucial piece of traditional jazz soloing. Blues licks and phrases can be inserted in many places you might not expect and are especially useful after the stage has been set by the other elements. To be stylistically appropriate these should not be aggressive blues-rock licks. Generally speaking if you use string bends larger than a half step, wide vibrato, distortion or other rock guitar sounds you're going into the direction of jazz-rock fusion instead of straight-ahead jazz. Fusion is great, but it's nice to be able to sound traditional if you're playing "The Days of Wine and Roses." Check out Wes Montgomery's version of that song on *Boss Guitar*, and notice the three or four places in his solo that keep it grounded with a little bit of blues.

The source materials for these licks are the same as in traditional blues:

1) The major pentatonic scale of the key center, B♭ in this example. We're sliding into the 3rd of the B♭ major pentatonic scale from a half-step below (and including the same blue note on the way down). It's harmonically correct to call the C♯ an augmented 9th in the key, but when blues is the context, conventional theory doesn't cleanly apply, so you might refer to this note as D♭, the minor 3rd in B♭. You don't need to try to hear it as a ♭9 over the Cm7 chord.

The major pentatonic scale with the ♯9 added is sometimes called the Country Blues or occasionally the "composite" blues scale. Notice in B♭ it's the same as the G minor blues scale, similar to the relative minor concept covered in Chapter 6, "Minor Scales and Harmony."

Minor pentatonic and the minor blues scale. This can work over minor tonic chords, minor blues progressions, and over traditional blues progressions, where the I, IV, and V are all dominant chords. Though strictly staying within this scale for an entire chorus probably means you're not playing jazz in the traditional sense, these licks are still important to know and mix in when the time's right.

2.

The ♭5 of the blues scale is a commonly-used dissonance over the IV7 in a blues progression. This example touches that note (F♭) twice, then descends to the 3rd of the chord.

3.

This cool pedal-tone blues lick works in multiple styles, and I probably use it too much!

4.

A double-stop blues lick for jazz, blues, or country.

5.

If licks are played with confidence, it's not always necessary that they follow every chord. If they're strong they'll float over the changes, add energy, and bring things home for your audience. By listening closely to your improvisations you'll likely hear what should be avoided, like hitting the 3rd of the I^7 over the IV^7 (a D on E♭^{7}).

The licks on this page are shown in their most obvious chordal context, but they can to some extent be forced onto other cadences in B♭ major or minor to your taste, e.g. over rhythm changes (Chapter 16).

Chapter 11: Lines on Longer Chords

▶ jsb11

Chord Tones on Strong Beats

Downbeats 1 and 3 in a measure are called the **strong** beats. The backbeats, 2 and 4, are weaker, but strong in comparison with the upbeat "ands."

$$|1 \quad \& \quad 2 \quad \& \quad 3 \quad \& \quad 4 \quad \& \quad |$$
$$S \quad w \quad s \quad w \quad S \quad w \quad s \quad w$$

In our earlier ii-V-I examples, each chord lasted for two beats. By starting down an 8th-note scale from any tone of the ii chord, you automatically hit tones of the chords that followed on beats 1 and 3.

When we start on the root of the ii chord (Am7 in the following examples), we get a chord tone on each change (beats 1 and 3). When starting from its 3rd, 5th, or 7th, we get chord tones on **all four** strong beats. Since we're looking at something we've played before, I'm going to add a new detail for you: a traditional extra tone, usually a chord factor, on an upbeat at the end of the line. This note should be short and unaccented (not too loud).

G Major Scale, Pattern 5, from A: root of iim7

G Major Scale, Pattern 5, from E: 5th of iim7

G Major Scale, Pattern 5, from C: 3rd of iim7

G Major Scale, Pattern 5, from G: 7th of iim7

Longer Chords

When a chord lasts for a full measure of 4/4 time or longer, a continuous eighth-note line that started with chord tones on the strong beats will sooner or later go through the root to the 7th. Non-chord tones will fall on strong beats from that point onward. When it's out of sync like this, it can sound like you are lost: getting to the next chord too soon, or landing on one that's not there. It may be as subtle as your line just feeling less energetic. If you can't hear this effect right away, that's OK. It may take some time before you start to compare the notes to the sound of the chord held in your head.

On the following page are some examples of how lines can go wrong in this way. We'll use the C major scale over Dm7. Let's try to hear the scale as D Dorian.

Examples of Weak and Potentially Confusing Lines

Descending scales and modes don't always work "as is" when a chord lasts for more than two beats.

D Dorian, Pattern 2, equal to C major Pattern 3

Dm⁷

tone:	D	C	B	A	G	F	E	D	C	B
degree:	1	m7	6	5	4	m3	2	1	m7	6

TAB: 7 5 4 / 7 5 / 8 7 5 / 8 7

Here, the listener may feel like there should have been a G7 chord on beat 3. The problem starts early in the line.

Dm⁷

tone:	F	E	D	C	B	A	G	F	E
degree:	m3	2	1	m7	6	5	4	m3	2

TAB: 6 5 / 7 5 4 / 7 5 / 8 7

Starting on the other chord tones, the same thing happens every time you cross the root-7th area (from D to C). Non-chord tones fall on the strong beats that follow.

When a line hits the 6th of a ii chord on beat 1 or 3, it can sound obviously wrong, because that note is also the 3rd of the V chord, the strongest implication of a move to that chord.

Dm⁷

tone:	A	G	F	E	D	C	B	A	G	F
degree:	5	4	m3	2	1	m7	6	5	4	m3

TAB: 5 8 6 5 / 7 5 4 / 7 5 / 8

This line for a static Dm7 is not bad but would be stronger if the G were not on beat 1 of the second measure.

Dm⁷

tone:	C	B	A	G	F	E	D	C	B
degree:	m7	6	5	4	m3	2	1	m7	6

TAB: 8 7 5 / 8 6 5 / 7 5 / 4

Because we are staying on Dm7, it's not so good that the 6th (B) on beat 1 is, again, implying a G7 chord that's not there.

If you keep playing down the scale, these lines will eventually right themselves so that chord tones fall on strong beats again, but only after a period that feels like it is stalling instead of moving forward. You can see that in the first example on this page. The C in measure 2 is a chord tone of Dm7.

Chromatic Passing Tones and Bebop Dorian

One way to fix the "stalling" problem is to add a chromatic tone between the root and the m7. This note pushes all the following ones later so chord tones fall on the strong beats. The tension of the non-chord tone on each weak beat is resolved on each strong beat, giving the line a sense of momentum.

D Bebop Dorian, Pattern 2

tone:	D	C♯	C♮	B	A	G	F	E	D	F
degree:	1	7	m7	6	5	4	m3	2	1	m3

Adding the chromatic note between root and 7th creates a **bebop** scale. The formerly seven-note scale now has eight notes and so more closely matches the rhythm of music in 4/4 time.

D Bebop Dorian, Pattern 2

tone:	F	E	D	D♭	C	B	A	G	F	D
degree:	3	2	1		7	6	5	4	3	1

As in the other diagrams, let's now go for simplicity over theoretically-correct naming. You'd probably call these passing tones major 7ths when describing them, and you could write them as C♯ notes followed by C♮ notes on the staff, but this way is easier to read. The idea of a ♭1 is kind of funny.

I'll also stop specifying the qualities of scale degrees. Assume the 3rd of a minor scale or chord is a minor 3rd, for example.

D Bebop Dorian, Pattern 1

tone:	A	G	F	E	D	D♭	C	B	A	F
degree:	5	4	3	2	1		7	6	5	3

When descending from the major 7th passing tone to the minor 7th on bebop scales, it can help you keep your place if you reach for the extra note with your pinky and slide right back into a familiar scale pattern. It also lets you slur onto the beat.

D Bebop Dorian, Pattern 2

tone:	C	B	A	G	F	E	D	D♭	C	A
degree:	7	6	5	4	3	2	1		7	5

The Bebop Dorian scale works ascending as well, but at first it's a good idea to focus on descending with it. Remember the extra passing tone is only there to correct the rhythmic feel of the line. Sometimes it is unnecessary, and may in fact throw things off.

We all know there are no hard rules in music. That said, here's the "wrong" way to apply chromatics. The D♭ is on a beat. Every tone in measure 1 from then on is an eighth note away from where we want it (although the second measure's E-D is cool on the m7 chord).

WRONG
Dm⁷

count: 1 & 2 & 3 & 4 & 1 & 2 & 3 & 4 &
D D♭ C B A G F E D

When the root is already on the upbeat, just follow with the usual seven-note scale instead. No passing tone is needed.

RIGHT
Dm⁷

count: 1 & 2 & 3 & 4 & 1 & 2 & 3 & 4 &
D C B A G F E D A

Here we're starting from the 3rd of the chord, this time on the "and" of beat 2. The passing tone is wrong, throwing the chord tones onto the upbeats.

WRONG
Dm⁷

count: 1 & 2 & 3 & 4 & 1 & 2 & 3 & 4 &
F E D D♭ C B A G F

Omit the passing tone if your descending line crosses from the root of the chord on an upbeat to the 7th on any downbeat.

RIGHT
Dm⁷

count: 1 & 2 & 3 & 4 & 1 & 2 & 3 & 4 &
F E D C B A G F C

Bebop Dominant

G Bebop Dominant Pattern 4 (C major Pattern 2)

Over static dominant chords, the most "inside" scale is Mixolydian. A chromatic tone between root and 7th can be applied the same as before, to place chord tones on strong beats. This modified Mixolydian mode is called **Bebop Dominant**.

G Bebop Dominant Pattern 5 (C major Pattern 3)

Here we start on B. The root, G on top of the staff, falls on beat 2. That's on a beat, so we add the passing tone after it so F falls on beat 3.

G Bebop Dominant Pattern 1 (C major Pattern 4)

This example starts a beat early from the G, adding more momentum to the line.

G Bebop Dominant Pattern 2 (C major Pattern 5)

As before, if you happen to play a root on an upbeat, leave out the passing tone if you want the line to fit the chord and keep moving. This line ends with a familiar jazz cliché.

G Bebop Dominant Pattern 3 (C major Pattern 1)

We can look for other good places to use a chromatic passing tone. Here a melodic jump sets up an opportunity to put one approaching the 5th (D) on beat 3 of measure 2.

In addition to the tone between root and m7 we can use other passing tones to correct a line that starts off (or goes) out of sync. A passing tone between the 4th and 3rd degrees are used here in an essential jazz lick.

G Dorian Pattern 4

Gm7

This example works the same way. If you've played a chord tone on an upbeat and there is enough time before the root-to-7 crossing point, you can add another passing tone for the same purpose, correcting the line in both places.

C Dorian Pattern 3

Cm7

With some experimentation you can find more places where it is appropriate to add chromatic tones to place chord tones on the beat. Try inserting them into every whole step in the scale, listening closely to decide which ones you prefer. If you want confirmation for your ears, look up Barry Harris's half-step rules.

F Dorian Pattern 2

Fm7

This line could be stopped earlier by changing the E♭♭ to D♭ and omitting the later notes.

B♭ Dorian Pattern 4

B♭m7

When starting on the 9th (2nd) degree of a chord, leave out the chromatic note; stay with the seven-note scale. This is a common scale exercise.

E♭ Dorian Pattern 1

E♭m7

Strategies for Major-Chord Lines

F major Pattern 1

1.

degree: 8 7 6 m6 5 4 3 2 1 5

B♭ major Pattern 4

2.

degree: 3 2 1 m7 7 6 5 4 3 1

E♭ major Pattern 2

3.

degree: 5 4 3 2 1 7 6 m6 5 3

A♭ major Pattern 5

4.

degree: 7 6 5 4 3 m2 2 1 7 5

D♭ major Pattern 3

5.

degree: 1 7 6 m6 5 4 3 2 1 5 7 1

The **Bebop Major** scale works somewhat the same as the others. Its added passing tone fills in the whole step between degrees 6 and 5. Again, the goal is to place chord tones on beats 1 and 3.

Static or long-lasting maj7 chords can be harder to navigate than the other types, partly because the root and 7th are only a half step apart. There is a potential clash when hitting the root over a maj7 chord, especially right on beat 1.

You can either avoid the root and aim for the 7th, or make sure that the chord has its 7th removed or is replaced by a 6th and/or 9th.

Example 1 on this page starts and finishes on the root of the chord, with the 5th on beat 3. To avoid a clash, the chord is just a major triad.

Example 2 starts on the 3rd of the chord. To keep the line swinging, the 7th on beat 3 is approached from a chromatic half-step below. Taken with the root on beat 2, these three notes are an *encirclement:* tones above and below the target. Classically speaking this is called a *double neighbor* figure. Encirclement can be applied to tones on other chord types that don't have the R-7 half-step problem.

Ex. 3: if the line keeps moving in the same direction toward resolution, the root on beat 3 is acceptable.

Ex. 4 has an encirclement of the 2nd degree on beat 4 in order to get the 7th on the next downbeat.

For Ex. 5, we'll make the chord a major 6th instead of maj7. This is often already the case when the melody of a song ends on the tonic (root) of the key. The two added notes in measure 2 reinforce the sense of finality.

This example has three phrases of four bars each, for a total of twelve bars. A three-note rhythmic motif starts line 1 and 2; line 3 varies it. Each is answered by variations on a 6-note motif that include chromatic tones applied according to the rhythmic guidelines we've studied on maj7 and m7 chords.

The first three measures are over a Gm7 chord, with a chromatic tone between steps 4 and 3 of the G Dorian mode. You can think of this as C Bebop Dominant applied to its related ii. This is pretty commonly used; just remember a passing major 3rd on a minor chord really must be on an upbeat.

Measure 4's line starts with a chord tone over a short ii-V, so no passing tone is needed. Measure 5 has the Bebop Major passing tone.

A partial Bebop Dorian scale appears in measure 7, with a complete Bebop Dominant line in measure 8. The E natural in measure 10 anticipates the key change to C major. This is another common jazz practice, approaching a chord tone from a half-step below, and in this case, riding a little ahead of a key change. Falling behind on them doesn't work nearly as well!

The final two measure's V7 and Imaj7 chords in C come early to create a syncopated figure, making it easy to hear we are at the end of the section and keep our places if it repeats.

Jazz Study #8: A Passing Remark

Improv Practice Assignment

Apply the practice routines described on p.22 and p.35 to the above chord progression.

12: Arpeggios in Major-Key Lines

▶ jsb12

Between scalar descents, a typical jazz line often ascends using arpeggios. The approach is the same for modal situations as for diatonic chords in a progression: Dorian (iim7), Mixolydian (V7), Ionian (Imaj7), and Lydian (IVmaj7). The basic guideline is to start from any chord tone and climb by 3rds within the appropriate scale, producing one of these groups of tones over the chord.

| 1 3 5 7 | 3 5 7 9 | 5 7 9 11 | 7 9 11 13 |

You can keep going, creating one big extended arpeggio (1 3 5 7 9 11, etc.), or repeating the same one an octave higher (e.g., 1 3 5 7, 8 10 12 15). You can also use smaller pieces of them and switch back into scalar movement when it sounds good to you.

V7 Chords

Learn to do this on dominant chords first. Playing the arpeggio that directly corresponds to the chord of the moment is good for sounding traditional, bluesy, and strong. It can be a little too "inside" in a jazz solo, especially if it has the root on a strong beat. (Ex. 1.)

To sound jazzier over a static G7 we can use Bm7♭5, Dm7, or Fmaj7, producing G9, G11, and G13, respectively. (Exs. 2-4)

You can think about these as diatonic substitutes. Remember that, for example, G7 is the V chord in the key of C. Arpeggios from this key, starting from each successive chord tone of G7, will give us successively higher extensions: 9th, 11th, and 13th.

The diatonic arpeggios for V7 lines:
- m7♭5 from the 3rd
- m7 from the 5th
- maj7 from the 7th (This one will also be used two ways on iim7 chords. Learn first for instant jazziness.)

As with scales, some arpeggio subs have things to look out for and possibly avoid, like placing the 11th on beat 1 or 3 over a maj7 chord.

66

For arpeggios over static minor 7th chords the default source is the Dorian mode. This way we will get a major 13th in our stack of extensions.

These examples are all in different keys so you can practice finding the related major key and listing its arpeggios.

A whole step down from the minor chord gives you the related major key. Once you find the related key, arpeggiate its diatonic chords from the 3rd, 5th, and 7th of the m7 chord.

In Ex.1, C#m7 is the ii chord in B major and we have one of that key's arpeggios, starting from E, the 3rd of the chord.

Exs. 2 (F#m7) and 3 (Bm7) approach beats 1 or 3 by scale, then ascend by diatonic arpeggio from the 5th or 7th.

You might think of Ex. 4 as two overlapping arpeggios from the key of D: Gmaj7 and Dmaj7, with a jump down an octave to keep in a playable range.

I've removed some of the slur markings from these examples because I want you to start remembering to add them on your own if you like the feeling they create.

Ex. 5 starts with a version of the 4-m3 jazz lick (D Bebop Dominant and A Bebop Dorian) from the previous chapter and adds the ascending arpeggio.

Learn your diatonic subs for iim7 lines:
• maj7 from the 3rd
• m7 from the 5th
• maj7 from the 7th

1. C#m7 (Emaj7 arpeggio) — 3 5 7 9

2. F#m7 (C#m7 arpeggio) — 5 7 9 11

3. Bm7 (Amaj7 arpeggio) — 7 9 11 13

4. Em7 (Gmaj7 arp—) (Dmaj7 arp—) — 3 5 7 9 11 13

5. Am7 (Gmaj7 arpeggio) — 7 9 11 13

Imaj7 Chords

1.

Cmaj7   pattern 2

3 5 7 1 3

2.

Cmaj7 pattern 3

5 7 1 3 5 7

3.

Cmaj7 pattern 4

7 1 3 5 7 1

4.

Cmaj7   (Em7 arpeggio)

3 5 7 9

5.

Cmaj7 (Bm7♭5 arpeggio)

7 9 11 13

6.

Cmaj7 (Dm7 arpeggio) (Gmaj)

9 11 13 1

In a major-key progression the Imaj7, maj6, or major triad is the tonic chord, usually coming at the end of a phrase. It's the place to resolve your line and leave some space. You may not feel the need for arpeggios much there. First try ascending with major pentatonic if you need to keep a line going.

Exs. 1-3:

With that said, the obvious starting places for the maj7 arpeggio are its 3rd, 5th, or 7th. Avoid placing the root on beats 1 or 3 if you can hear the major 7th in the same octave in the accompaniment. (Conversely, if the I chord is a maj6 or just a triad, you might prefer to resolve to the root in your line.)

Ex. 4

The most common diatonic substitute arpeggio for a tonic maj7 chord is a m7 from the 3rd, providing the 9th of the chord. Note the Vmaj triad (G here) is contained within iiim7.

Ex.5

Avoid placing the 11th (same as the 4th) on the strongest beats of a major chord. By starting a m7♭5 arpeggio from the 7th degree on beat 1 or 3 you get the 11th on beat 2 or 4.

Ex. 6

The 9th can also sound good on the downbeat over the maj7 chord. Here's iim7 over the I chord, followed by a descending V triad.

This lesson's major subs:
- m7 from the 3rd
- maj triad from the 5th
- m7♭5 from the 7th
- m7 from the 9th

The Lydian mode is the first scale choice on IVmaj7 in a major key and on most **non-diatonic maj7 chords** like the non-diatonic Fmaj7 chord on p.41. It replaces the potentially dissonant 4th degree with the $\sharp$4.

We can include this note (as the $\sharp$11) in the stack of extensions for a maj7 with these arpeggios:

- maj7 from the 5th
- m7 from the 7th
- m7 arpeggio from the 3rd works the same as it does on Imaj7

Similar use of arpeggios will work on the diatonic chords that we haven't covered: iii, vi, and vii. A few notes:

• When a iiim7 chord occurs within a major key progression you could use a diatonic arpeggio from its root or 3rd. The iii chord is often part of a iii-vi-ii-V or similar progression. It's in the tonic family and shares many tones with Imaj7, so some phrases you'd use on Imaj7 that start on a common tone with iii would also work there., but be aware the tonic on a strong beat may clash with the iii chord's 5th.

• vim7 chord: diatonic arpeggios from its m3rd and 5th work best. Avoid placing its $\flat$13 on a strong beat. vim7 is in the tonic family so it can be treated as if it were Imaj7, e.g. over Am7 play what you'd play over Cmaj7.

• When m7$\flat$5 chords appear they are almost always part of a minor-key ii-V. Diatonic arpeggios from any chord tone will work. This chord can take a lot of tension, because it's going to move.

The examples in this chapter used *close-voiced* ascending arpeggios almost exclusively (the notes are always arranged 1-3-5-7), but they can of course have some skipped notes, or be played descending, broken into pieces, and/or sequenced into patterns.

On the next page is a jazz study that applies some of what we've covered.

We've got arpeggios hitting extensions in measures 2, 5, 10, and 12. Alternatives to passing tones for placing chord tones on strong beats are explored: skips, repeated 8ths, and quarter notes. Measures 15 and 16 have a commonly-used reference to Gershwin's "Fascinating Rhythm."

When chords last long enough it is useful to consider them in modal terms. Each chord getting its own scale is called the **chord-scale** system. Combined with the key-center approach it helps us see which notes are chord tones and which are extensions, where chromaticism will work, and where licks we know can be plugged in, along with creating long smooth arcs of melody.

Jazz Study #9: Accept All Substitutes

C Mixolydian

Cm⁷   F⁷   Cm⁷   F⁷

B♭ Major
= C Dorian   = F Mixolydian

Fm⁷   B♭⁷   Gm⁷   C⁷

E♭ Major
= F Dorian   = B♭ Mixolydian   F Major / = G Dorian   = C Mixolydian

Fm⁷   B♭⁷   Fm⁷   B♭⁷   B♭m⁷   E♭⁷   C⁷

E♭ Major   A♭ Major / =B♭ Dorian   =E♭ Mixolydian

Improv Practice

Apply arpeggio connection and scalar chord-tone targeting on the above chord progression. You can target multiple tones for the static C7 chord, or use motific development.

Chapter 13: Long ii-V-Is

Major-Key Lines

Over a four-measure chord phrase, a typical jazz line is about three measures long, leaving a little space at the end for breathing room or a pickup into the next idea. In this longer line there will be time for direction changes, arpeggios, interval skips, and rhythmic variations.

As before we'll use chromatic tones on upbeats, usually placing chord tones on beats 1 and 3 of the measure.

ii-V Shared Arpeggios

The iim7 and V7 chords share some arpeggios that work in both places, making it a little easier to ascend over either. Over both Dm7 and G7 (ii-V in C major), you can start from any beat and arpeggiate:

- Dm7 (iim7)
- Fmaj7 (IVmaj7)

Over the ii chord, those are arpeggios from root or 3rd, diatonic to the key. Over the V, they're arpeggios from 5th and 7th. In short: iim7 and IVmaj7 arps over either chord of a major ii-V.

This first example uses the shared IV (Fmaj7) arpeggio over both chords to get extended chord sounds: Dm9, G13.

Next we have a chromatic pickup to the root of the iim7 in G. There's a triplet Am9 arpeggio in measure 2, that reaches the 13th of D. The iim9 arp includes both shared arpeggios, iim7 connected to IVmaj7. If you are swinging the eighth notes, the triplet will come pretty naturally. A Bm7 arp ascends over Gmaj7.

This line in Pattern 1 of F has a triplet arpeggio as a pickup. The line breaks for a rhythmic idea in measure 2 and resumes with an Am triad over Fmaj7, then the bebop major scale.

A pickup from the "and" of 3 is followed by chromatic approaches to chord tones on a major ii-V-I in B♭.

The back door cadence (ivm7-♭VII7-Imaj7) switches from B♭ minor to B♭ major by using a ii-V in D♭, the relative major of the starting minor key. It may seem complicated on paper, but it's a commonly-used chord move. The easiest way to improvise here is to use the B♭ minor scale for the first two measures, then switch to B♭ major. The example line uses descending arpeggio subs with a similar fretboard shape.

Assignment

Write out five of your own 4-measure ii-V-I lines using major scales with appropriate chromaticism and different arpeggio substitutes from Chapter 11. Record them over a backing track, then listen to the results. Evaluate them for thematic continuity and forward movement.

Earlier we used the natural minor scale over minor-key progressions, only switching to the harmonic minor scale over the V7 chord. The minor pentatonic and blues scales are also of course important to have ready to apply in minor-key situations. They're an essential part of the jazz style and can work well over any of the chords of a minor progression.

Dorian vs. Aeolian on the Tonic Minor (im)

You can switch to Dorian on the im chord in a diatonic minor progression, treating it as if it were a static chord and using the same arpeggios as in Chapter 12 (p.67, 70).

The decision to make the switch from natural minor depends on the timing of the 6th degree. If it is on a weak beat (measure 3, "and" of beat 2 here), the minor 6th degree might sound more appropriate, especially if the chords are moving.

On a strong beat or as a sustained pitch (and of course over a static chord), the Dorian scale's major 6th will usually sound like a better fit. This phrase wouldn't make much sense with A♭ instead of A♮ in m.3.

You can also use both notes in succession.

You'll quickly notice it's not a good idea to use the A natural (except as a passing tone) over the other chords in a diatonic C minor progression.

im/maj7

As a special case, the i chord's quality can be minor/major7. Here are the tones in a Cm/maj7 chord.

$$C \quad E\flat \quad G \quad B$$
$$1 \quad m3 \quad 5 \quad 7$$

The most familiar place for this chord is in the linear cliché: Cm Cm/maj7 Cm7 Cm6, where the descending line (C-B-B♭-A) can be in any voice. A fancier name for this is "chromatic embellishment of static harmony" (CESH). If these notes are already being played by another instrument, your line will usually not need to hit them and might sound better targeting the 3rd, 5th, or 9th.

If your playing does cross the chromatic line, of course, it shouldn't clash. For that reason it's recommended to practice hitting those notes but then also practice moving in another direction.

Although you might get by over the m/maj7 chord with the harmonic minor scale, its best fit is usually the **melodic minor** scale: 1 2 m3 4 5 6 7. Here are five patterns with position marks in Dm.

Melodic Minor Scale

Pattern 1 (2fr) — Pattern 2 (4fr) — Pattern 3 (6fr) — Pattern 4 (9fr) — Pattern 5 (11fr)

Melodic minor differs by one note from Dorian, Harmonic Minor, and the major scale, so you might start off thinking of it as a variation of any one of these. You'll want to get this scale under your fingers for its important modal applications, but don't rush into it at the expense of the major scale and its modes.

If the i chord is just a tonic minor triad or a m(add9) you can try interpreting it as minor/major7 as in Miles Davis's "Solar," which contains the maj7 in the melody. The key changes to Fmaj in m.3.

When it is part of a progression (usually a minor ii ∅-V), the dissonance and tension of the iim7♭5 chord allows us to run a natural minor scale line over it with any tone on a strong beat, even its ♭6th degree (e.g. B♭ over Dm7♭5). This means we don't really need a chromatic passing tone from root to 7th over this chord.

An 11th in the melody sounds great over the m7♭5 chord. It can seem like a composer or soloist sets out from the beginning to make their melody fall on this tone (m.4 of "Here's That Rainy Day," m.13 of "Love For Sale," m.8 & 10 of "Gloria's Step").

A non-diatonic major 9th extension can be used for color on this chord, especially on ballads. This example has a chromatically descending voice from E-E♭-D spread across measures 1-3 .

Being familiar with the m7♭5 arpeggio from any of its tones lets you nail the chord and also use it in its important role as a substitution. Arpeggiation through upper extensions (♭9 or ♮9, 11, ♭13) over the m7♭5 is possible but more than we need to tackle in a book of basics. If you're ready for it, however, start working on arpeggios of the harmonized F melodic minor scale. Its sixth mode is D Locrian ♯2.

V7♭9 in Minor

The previous observation about the iim7♭5 chord—that a natural minor scale can be phrased with any note on any beat over it—applies to the V7 in minor as well, except that you may want to avoid placing the tonic of the key on a strong beat at first.

For our first arpeggiation over the V7 in minor keys, let's start with the 7♭9 arpeggio only, using the same notes in any octave (no 11ths or 13ths for now). When you play this arpeggio from each of its tones, notice that the 3rd, 5th, ♭7th, and ♭9th are all minor 3rds apart, forming a diminished arpeggio. When only these notes are played, the arpeggio shapes are similar all over the fretboard.

Pattern 1 | Pattern 2 | Pattern 3 | Pattern 4 | Pattern 5

ii∅-V-i Lines

This has arpeggiation of the iim7♭5 chord. Note the mixture of natural and harmonic minor on the V7.

This one uses 7♭9 arpeggiation on the V7 chord.

Sixteenth-Note Lines

If you can cleanly play fast enough and/or the song tempo is slow enough, most eighth-note lines in this book that fit a long ii-V will fit a short ii-V if you play in sixteenth notes: four notes per beat. The sixteenth notes feel pretty straight; they only need to bounce if you're playing on a sixteenth-note shuffle groove (think hip-hop).

Here's a line with sixteenth notes over a long minor ii-V-i. Obviously this means there is room for more complicated ideas. This example has a sequenced arpeggio in measure 2. When played in eighth notes this example would have two measures per chord, and would start on beat 2.

Speaking of sixteenth notes, with room on a static chord you can get a little more adventurous with chromaticism to create some tension before going back inside. This also would work as 8ths on four measures of an uptempo D7 vamp, starting on the "and" of beat 4.

Chapter 14: Jazz Blues

▶ jsb14

There are many variations on the blues progression. For typical blues tunes like "Straight No Chaser," "Twisted," "Blues In The Closet," or "Sandu," the main melody could have specific chords that fit the composition, but then the solo sections may contain chords that the soloists prefer (*blowing* changes). In this chapter we'll start with a simple blues progression and dress it up step by step until we get a version of jazz blues chord changes that is often used for solos.

A basic blues progression is 12 bars long and only uses three chords: the I, IV, and V in a single key.

|I |I |I |I |

|IV |IV |I |I |

|V |IV |I |V   ‖

We'll write out the chords in the key of B♭ at first because this is a common key for horn players and the key of most blues tunes in fakebooks. You'll want to memorize the progression(s) in at least C, F, and E♭ and of course the guitar-friendly keys of E, A, D, and G.

First we'll make all three chords dominant sevenths. By classical Western harmony this is no longer a diatonic progression (because there's no single scale from which all the chords are derived) but we are going to say it's all in the key of B♭.

|B♭7 |B♭7 |B♭7 |B♭7 |

|E♭7 |E♭7 |B♭7 |B♭7 |

|F7 |E♭7 |B♭7 |F7   ‖

You probably know you can feel your way through this by using the B♭ minor pentatonic scale for an entire solo. Not every note is theoretically in line with the harmony, but that's good in the down-home blues. You'll just notice if you listen closely that it sounds better if you are careful about emphasizing some of the scale tones over some chords. For example, I try not to play the tonic note of the scale (B♭) right on the downbeat of the F7 chord. Besides the obvious clash, I want to create a sense of movement toward that note on the chord that comes after F7.

The twelve-bar form is divided into three four-bar phrases. Part of our job when soloing is to follow (and make the listener feel) that phrase length by resolving around beat 1 of measures 4, 8, and 12. You can stop playing and leave some breathing room in these places, or play a long note and let it ring before starting the next phrase. As you get used to implying these resolution points in your solo, you can get the job done with your note selection even if the line is continuous.

Measure 11 can also be heard as a resolution point for the entire form. Hitting the tonic note here is a good idea, but you don't have to stop; you may want to continue your line into measure 12. Measures 11 and 12 are called the *turnaround* bars. The chords here create the expectation that the progression is going to start over. If your solo will continue, you can use bar 12 to get an early start into the next chorus with a pickup phrase. If

77

another instrument or vocal will take over, then it may be best to finish in bar 11 and give them some room.

It can be hard to keep track of exactly where you are in a progression if you haven't practiced counting bars much. Make sure you can actually count aloud through all twelve bars. You don't have to count all four beats in each bar. Just call out the downbeats, 1 through 12. For now, prioritize the counting (and tapping your foot) over the playing. Play as little as needed to make sure you're keeping your place at all times. When you do play, keep it very simple, using lots of quarter notes and space, and remember the natural resolution points in bars 4, 8, and 12. I suggest just stopping on B♭ in bars 4, 8, and 11, then on F in bar 12.

I don't really want you to memorize this next example. Just read through it a couple times and play along, then try to improvise something rhythmically solid and very simple while making sure to count aloud. Just use the one scale at first so you can isolate the counting skill. You can play far less than I did if necessary. If something drops out, make it the playing. Counting will teach you to keep your place better than anything else.

Count every bar aloud and improvise something simple like this.

If you want an example of someone playing great solos with just these notes no matter what the chords are, you can't go wrong with Albert King's 1967 album *Born Under A Bad Sign.*

"Jump Blues" cats of the 40s (T-Bone Walker, Louis Jordan, etc.) played V7 in measures 9 and 10, with the bassist (and/or the pianist's left hand) walking up from C in bar 9. Jump blues also often had a major 6th chord for the I, and was even more harmonically simple, with no turnaround in measures 11 and 12.

While the chords may have been fairly straightforward, players still reached for extensions and dissonant blue notes in their solos. Here's an example that's similar to the T-Bone classic "Strollin' With Bone."

Jazz Study #10: Jump Blues

As we gradually make the progression jazzier, we'll add back the scales and targeting of chord tones, but try to remember the phrase lengths, even if we are playing lines that cross the phrase boundaries.

Improv Practice

Apply arpeggiation (p.22) and chord-tone targeting (p. 36) to the above chord progression. After hitting a chord tone, target the occasional 6th or 9th of the chord on beat 1 or 3 as I did in measures 1, 6, and 12.

Jazzing Up the Blues Progression

First we'll add a *quick change* to the IV chord in measure 2. This is often done to accommodate a melody or just to add some variety.

You can hear a great example of the quick change in "Honky Tonk" (Parts 1 & 2) by Bill Doggett, from 1956, with Billy Butler on guitar.

Next, a #IVdim7 chord may be used in measure 6. This is very traditional; other chord moves have been placed here to update the vibe (e.g. E♭m7 A♭7), but we still need to be familiar with this chord. Notice the Edim7 (E°7) chord differs from E♭7 by just one note. Only the root has changed. The new note is also the "blue note" of the B♭ blues scale. In this measure it usually sounds good to use an E in the solo instead of (or in addition to, depending on the timing) the E♭.

For bars 9 and 10 we'll use a ii-V, making the inverted V in the jump blues into a diatonic iim7 chord. Because we're heading in the jazz direction, we'll use I-VI-ii-V in the turnaround measures (11-12).

Here are a few different turnaround progressions and licks, shown in the key of C to make them easier to understand and transpose.

There are many variations on the turnaround bars. Because the turnaround chords are short (and the progression might go at a high tempo), players often transcribe, steal, trade, and practice licks that fit them.

It will often feel more natural to finish your phrase by measure 11 of the blues. Let the turnaround chords speak for themselves, and use the space to get ready for another chorus.

Turnaround licks are nonetheless good to know, because they can be substituted in other progressions, for example when there are two measures on a tonic chord followed by key change up a fourth, among other possibilities.

Original progression

| Dm^7 | G^7 | $Cmaj^7$ | | Gm^7 | C^7 | $Fmaj^7$ | |

After reharmonization with turnaround

| Dm^7 | G^7 | $Cmaj^7$ A^7 | Dm^7 G^7 Gm^7 | C^7 | $Fmaj^7$ | |

Our blues is sounding jazzier. The last change we'll make to get a stock jazz blues is to increase the momentum into the phrases that start in measures 5 and 9 by adding major ii-Vs in measures 4 and 8. Here is the final product with a sample solo. Measure 9 quotes Matthew Gee's "Oh Gee."

Jazz Study #11: B♭ Blues

There are of course many more variations on this basic 12-bar platform but this one is very common and a good place to start.

You might wonder: if we are setting up the Cm in measure 9 with a ii-V in measure 8, why isn't this bar Dm7♭5 - G7? It would make sense: a minor ii-V-i. And the previous measure's B♭7 contains the A♭ that's also in Dm7♭5. Nonetheless Dm7 (the diatonic iiim7 chord in B♭) sounds better and is the one that gets used in this measure of the jazz blues most often. The ear is the boss.

Improv Practice

Apply the practice steps to the jazz blues. Keep this progression in your practice schedule indefinitely, making it fresh by adding challenges to the linear approaches, adding keys and positions, learning new blues heads, etc.

Chapter 15: Altered Dominants

The 5th mode of harmonic minor gives us the extensions ♭9, 11, and ♭13 (equal to ♯5) over the V7 chord in a minor key. Here's G harmonic minor over D7. (Sometimes this sound is called *Phrygian Dominant*, although that name more closely applies to static situations and other styles.)

G harmonic minor scale = D (Phrygian Dominant)   D7   Gm

R ♭2 3 4 5 ♭6 ♭7   R 3 5 ♭7 ♭9 11 ♭13

Compared to harmonic minor, the *altered* scale—mode 7 of the melodic minor scale—creates more tension over the dominant chord, partly by avoiding the root of the tonic chord (thus saving it for the resolution). Notice it contains the tones on either side of the upcoming tonic, a half-step above (♭5) and below (3).

E♭ melodic minor scale = D altered   D7alt   Gm

R 2 ♭3 4 5 6 7   R ♭2 ♭3 ♭4 ♭5 ♭6 ♭7   R 3 ♯5 ♭7 ♭9 ♯9 ♭5

A dominant chord in this situation usually has only the original root, major 3rd and minor 7th. Any other tones are altered. By convention the altered tones are called ♭5, ♯5, ♭9, and ♯9 as in measure 3 above. This is how you'll see them written in chord names when these extensions are desired. In a written melody or lick it can be easier to read if the notes are written as their enharmonic equivalents as in measure 2 above, although it can go either way.

Here are five patterns of the altered scale to cover the fretboard. We can refer to the 9ths as 2nds in the scale. These patterns are in D so that they can be shown in order from Pattern 1 to Pattern 5, with no open-string notes. D altered = E♭ melodic minor. Melodic minor up a half step is how many guitarists find it.

Pattern 1	Pattern 2	Pattern 3	Pattern 4	Pattern 5

Pattern 1 (3fr): ♭7 ♯2 ♯5 1 / ♭5 3 ♭2 ♭5 / 1 ♭7 / ♯5 ♭2 ♭5 ♯2 ♯5 / 3

Pattern 2 (5fr): 1 ♭7 / ♯5 ♭2 ♭5 ♯2 ♯5 / 1 3 / ♭7 ♯2 ♯5 ♭2 ♭7 / 3 ♭5

Pattern 3 (7fr): 1 / ♭7 ♯2 ♯5 ♭2 ♭7 / 3 ♭5 / 1 ♭7 ♯2 1 / ♭2 ♭5 3 ♯5 ♭2

Pattern 4 (10fr): 1 ♭7 ♯2 1 / ♭2 ♭5 3 ♯5 ♭2 / 1 / ♯2 ♯5 ♭2 ♭5 ♭7 ♯2 / 3

Pattern 5 (12fr): 1 / ♯2 ♯5 ♭2 ♭5 ♭7 ♯2 / 3 3 / ♭7 ♯2 ♯5 1 / ♭5 3 ♭2 ♭5

If the chord name says D7alt, D7#5♭9, or D7#5#9, and sometimes D7♭5, D7#5, D7♭9 and D7#9, then:

- any of the altered notes may be used in the chord,
- no perfect 5ths or natural 9ths should be present, and
- the altered scale is phrased over it.

The typical application of the altered chord and scale is V7 in a minor key. Often the alteration is not specified on the chart. It's up to you to interpret from the chords and your ear that you have a ii∅-V-i or other situation where it makes sense for a dominant chord to be altered. When providing accompaniment, if you're not sure, play any dominant chord as a shell, without its 5th, so the soloist has freedom to alter or not as they see fit.

Am7♭5   D7   Gm

Common ways to get altered upper extensions on a dominant chord are to play:
- a mi/maj7 or mi/maj9 arpeggio a half-step above the root, e.g., B♭m/maj7 over A7;
- a m7♭5 arpeggio a whole-step below the root, e.g. Fm7♭5 over G7.

Both are included in the next example. In addition to the V7 chord in minor keys, you can try using altered scales or arpeggios over **any** dominant chord that resolves up a fourth; for example, over a *secondary dominant* chord like A7 in the key of C (the V7 of ii—"five of two"). Alteration can also happen on the V7 in a major key here, although your line must be back in C major on the next downbeat.

C   A7#5   Dm7   G7   C

(B♭m/maj7 arp)   (Fm7♭5 arp--)

We'll see more about secondary dominant chords in the next chapter. They get extensive coverage in the book *Harmonic Minor, Melodic Minor, and Diminished Scales for Guitar*, along with all the modes of melodic minor and their usual applications.

In the case of Cole Porter's "I Love You" a minor ii⌀-V7 resolves to a major I chord. The switch from altered back to major can be striking. Here's a line for those changes:

Minor Blues

Some examples of minor blues in the jazz realm are "Mr. P.C.," "Footprints," "Stolen Moments," and "Equinox." Here's a basic 12-bar form.

im	%	%	%
ivm	%	%	%
♭VImaj7	V7	im	%

The im and ivm may be triads, m7, or m6 chords, and may have the CESH or another linear scheme.

Sort of like in the jazz blues from Chapter 14, the minor blues has countless possible variations, including a quick change to ivm in measure 2, setup ii⌀-Vs, and some type of turnaround at the end. Measure 9 can be a iim7♭5 chord. Here's a version of how it might go in A minor, though I should tell you that this is not a universally recognized set of blowing changes the way the jazz blues is.

Am7	Dm7	Am7	Em7♭5 A7
Dm7	Dm7	Am7 Am/G	F♯m7♭5 B7
Bm7♭5	E7	Am7	Bm7♭5 E7

In practice, minor blues progressions may be a little more open-sounding, with fewer extra chord changes. Players may change up the chords from one chorus to the next with embellishments they know, agree upon, or hear on the spot.

The usual scales are natural minor and the blues scale. The Dorian mode is used more often than not on the respective i and iv chords to get the major 6th, jazzier-sounding than the diatonic minor 6th.

Harmonic minor on dominant chords may be used but is not always necessary. You should know it, but don't overuse it if you want to stay bluesy. The same can be said of the altered scale.

The following minor blues example sounds best to me with a medium to uptempo swing feel, but it could also work as a straight eighth-note Latin, or 60s cool jazz like "Little Sunflower" or "Cantaloupe Island."

Sevenths, ninths, elevenths, and thirteenths are emphasized over the minor chords. These extensions are all easy to hear as the minor chords last for awhile each time they appear. All the phrases in the example end on upbeats where it's easier to make extensions work.

In measure 9 the E7-F7 move makes the A blues scale sound strong if it's done right. The 7th of F7 (E♭) is the ♭5 or blue note of Am.

Jazz Study #12: Minor Blues

For the solo over these blues, we'll move up to Pattern 5 of A minor. You could stay in Pattern 4 but measures 9-10 might be awkward to play.

A Dexter Gordon-style starting phrase grabs the listener's attention with emphasis on the 9th and 13th. A Bm arpeggio in measures 3 and 4 supports extensions and targets the 5th of Dm7 in measure 5. From here there's a bop line that skips the root of the chord on the way down. The sharped notes in bars 6, 9, and 10 are chromatic neighbor tones.

A G triad in measure 8 targets the E7 in bar 9 and also starts a blues lick. The G$\sharp$ at the end of bar 10 sounds less like an obvious harmonic minor resolution to A in measure 11 when used with the B as an encirclement.

Jazz Study #13: Minor Blues Solo

Improv Practice

Make the minor blues the subject of your improv practice, mixing up chord tones, extensions, blues licks and motific development. Also add some variations to the progression, like a iim7$\flat$5 in measures 9, which will create an opportunity to play a long minor ii-V-i line.

Chapter 16: Rhythm Changes

▶ jsb16

Rhythm changes refers to the chord progression to Gershwin's "I Got Rhythm," variations of which are used in "Anthropology," "Cotton Tail," and "Oleo," among others. Like the blues, this timeless progression (especially important in the bebop era of the 1940s-50s) is an essential platform for improvisation that, when practiced, helps develop your ability to play over others.

The overall 32-bar form is AABA. I-vi-ii-V7 cadences start each A section, with a I-IV move in bars 5 and 6. In the version we'll practice here, we have iii-VI7-ii-V7 at the end of lines 1, 2, 3, and 7.

The B section is a very common "middle 8": a cycle of fourths with dominant chords for two measures each: III7, VI7, II7, V7. The final A section resembles the second A section, possibly with a different ending.

It's a good idea to work this out in all twelve keys. Here's our common version in B♭.

| B♭ Gm7 | Cm7 F7 | Dm7 G7 | Cm7 F7 |

| B♭ B♭7 | E♭ E°7 | Dm7 G7 | Cm7 F7 ‖

| B♭ Gm7 | Cm7 F7 | Dm7 G7 | Cm7 F7 |

| B♭ B♭7 | E♭ E°7 | Cm7 F7 | B♭   ‖

| D7 | ⁄. | G7 | ⁄. |

| C7 | ⁄. | F7 | Cm7 F7 ‖

| B♭ Gm7 | Cm7 F7 | Dm7 G7 | Cm7 F7 |

| B♭ B♭7 | E♭ E°7 | Cm7 F7 | B♭   ‖

Practice Chunks

The A sections contain four unique two-bar progressions.

1. | B♭ Gm7 | Cm7 F7 | ‖   (I-vi-ii-V)

2. | Dm7 G7 | Cm7 F7 | ‖   (iii-VI-ii-V)

3. | B♭ B♭7 | E♭ E°7 | ‖   (I-I7-IV-♯IV°7)

4. | Cm7 F7 | B♭ | ‖   (a short ii-V-I)

Apportion your practice time so that you get five minutes on each two-bar chunk. You will only see serious improvement over weeks or months, so don't overdo any one thing in a single sitting.

Everything we've learned so far in this book may be applied to these changes. Because the A-section chords change quickly and are predictably familiar, you can mix in **a few** ideas that float over the changes, playing blues licks or almost anything in $B\flat$ that sounds catchy even if it has non-chord tones on the strong beats. Think of this advice more as an opportunity for variety than as an excuse to ignore the changes.

Chunk 1. I-vi-ii-V: |B♭ Gm7 |Cm7 F7 |

Generally speaking you can do what we've done before:

- Target chord tones in major-key lines, with the respective bebop chromaticism
- Use diatonic substitute arpeggios starting on each chord tone
- State and develop rhythmic/melodic motifs
- Force alterations over the V7 shell.

If the G were dominant here instead of minor (and in some tunes it is) this would be the most common jazz blues turnaround. Some licks used in that situation will also sound good here.

89

Chunk 2. iii-VI-ii-V: |Dm7   G7 |Cm7 F7 |

For some tunes, measure 3 of the progression is identical to meas. 1. In this version we have Dm7-G7. Don't think of this as a ii-V in C major. It sounds smoother to continue using B$\flat$ major over Dm7 as before with G7 functioning as the V of ii as in Chapter 15, Altered Dominants.

For the VI7 (G7, the V of ii in B$\flat$ here), you can use:
- C harmonic minor or the G altered scale
- 7$\flat$9 arpeggios
- m/maj7 or m/maj9 arpeggios up a half step (A$\flat$m/maj9)
- more B$\flat$ major or blues.

Now let's loop measures 5-6.

etc.

Chunk 4. ii-V-I: |Cm7   F7 |B♭ |

(In the first A section, measures 7-8 are the same as 3-4.) In the second and the final A sections there are short ii-V-Is. I think you already know what to do here.

Bigger Chunks

Once you've practiced the small sections many times, gradually hook them together in longer loops. Repeat and/or develop some of your ideas into longer phrases. Here are some examples for measures 5-8.

As four-bar phrases start to reach the level where you can pull them off if you concentrate ("conscious competence"), add full eight-bar sections where ideas are connected.

(continued on next page)

Bb   Bb7   Eb   E°7   Dm7   G7   Cm7   F7

(musical notation and TAB)

The B Section

This section gives you lots of freedom. The dominant chords are long enough to be interpreted as static if you prefer, so you could play Mixolydian or blues-based ideas on each. You can also change any two-bar phrase to a major-key ii-V7: |Am7 | D7 | instead of D7 for two measures, etc.

I think you already know how to solo in two- and four-bar phrases on static dominant chords with these approaches, which would work just fine. Instead of that, however, in the example I try to treat the chords as a series of secondary dominants in the original key. In order to keep the feeling of Bb as the overall key center, you can't loop one of these chords for long, so I'll work on the whole eight measures at once. When it's up to tempo you can hear it how it works as a bridge, temporarily departing from the key of Bb yet still inexorably marching back to it.

A dominant chord has what you might call an "intended target" chord: the diatonic chord a fourth higher. Within one key, there are minor targets (ii, iii, vi), and major ones (I, IV, V). If the intended target has a minor third, you can use harmonic minor or the altered scale on the dominant. If its intended target has a major 3rd, first try a scale that contains that note, like Mixolydian, bebop dominant, or major blues. Remember, you're not just looking at the quality of the chord that follows on the chart, because that may be non-diatonic. You're remembering what it would be if **were** diatonic.

D7   G7

Bb: V/vi   V/ii
G harmonic minor   C harmonic minor

(musical notation and TAB)

C7   F7   Cm7   F7

V/V   V   iim7   V7
C Bebop Dominant   Bb major w/ chromatic encirclements

(musical notation and TAB)

Another way to think about the B section is to keep as many notes from the B♭ major scale as possible and only change it to accommodate the non-diatonic notes in the chords. You'll get the following scales as a result. They're almost the same as in the previous strategy.

D7: B♭ C D E♭ **F♯** G A   (G harmonic minor)
G7: **B** C D E♭ F G A   (C melodic minor)
C7: B♭ C D **E** F G A   (C Mixolydian)
F7: B♭ C D E♭ F G A   (B♭ major)

Keep hooking together pieces until you are soloing over the 32-bar form. It's also a good idea to practice any tricky transitions between phrases and sections. In this progression, that might be the last two measures of the A section going into the first two measures of the B section. This sample solo starts with a quote from the *Flintstones* theme.

Jazz Study #14: Rhythm Changes solo

If you're repeating the entire form you will be playing the A section three times in a row, which can make it easy to lose your place. Try to use your own phrasing to help define the form for yourself, the band, and the audience. Consider concluding your chorus of solo with a clear resolution in measure 31. If you plan to take another chorus, you'll have the space to start it with a pickup phrase in measure 32.

As this type of form and progression becomes more familiar, the band may push the boundaries, but everyone shares some responsibility for spelling things out. You'll hear versions where everyone starts out together but soon are just keeping the original form and basic changes in their heads for reference. No matter how wild it may sound, it's almost never a free-for-all random jam.

Improv Practice

Apply improv techniques to rhythm changes in successively larger chunks as described in this chapter. This is another progression to keep on the schedule for a long time.

Chapter 17: Form And Pacing

Our final chapter has a longer sample solo that incorporates many of the topics we've covered. The chords are based on a jazz standard. As in rhythm changes, the form is AABA. This time, however, each section is 16 bars, for a total of 64. When you have a solo as long as/longer than this, you want to try for a contour of energy, where simpler ideas are used first so you have some room to build. Try to save the more complicated or energetic ideas and higher pitches for a climax point somewhere in the second half. Here that point is probably in the last half of the B section. The final A section tapers off a bit but still has some interesting lines alternating with blues licks.

Look at the chords first, finding key centers and the minimum necessary scales. Later you can add more possibilities. On the facing page is the chart with just chords, harmonic analysis, and some suggestions for non-diatonic scales. To save space it uses standard "road map" directions:

- Repeat signs on the A section
- Single-measure repeat signs: %
- D.C. al Fine—*da capo*, Italian for "from head" (back to the top), *al fine*—"to the end"
- Stop when you see the word *fine*, but only because the previous *al fine* instruction told you to.

The result of these instructions is the AABA form, after which you could play it all again, with some or all band members taking solos, trading phrases with the drummer, and finally having the leader cue the final melody with a clear nod or literally tapping his/her head.

$B^\flat$ blues lines work well over the IV7-I7 vamp and also on the ii$^{\emptyset}$7-V7-im that ends the A sections. The third line of the A sections is a major ii-V-I with a IV7 at the end. Just changing the F natural in $D^\flat$ major to $F^\flat$ to follow the chord creates $D^\flat$ melodic minor, the fourth mode of which is $G^\flat$ Lydian Dominant or Lydian Flat Seven.

The B section starts with another ii-V-I, this time with $B^\flat$7 (V7 of ii) in its 4th measure (measure 36 of the solo). $E^\flat$ harmonic or natural minor or the $B^\flat$ altered scale work on that measure. The same applies to the V7 of the key change to $E^\flat$m in measure 41. Consecutive ii-Vs in F minor and $E^\flat$ minor set up the return to the A section.

The second A section in the sample solo quotes the riff from Donald Byrd's "Sudwest Funk."

A

E^{b7} ⸬ | | ./. | B^{b7} | | ./. |

B^b: IV7   I7

| E^{b7} | | ./. | B^{b7} | | ./. |

IV7   I7

D♭ melodic minor

| E^bm^7 | A^{b7} | $D^b maj^7$ | G^{b7} | |

D^b: ii-7   V7   Imaj7   IV7

fine

| Cm^{7b5} | F^7 | B^bm | | ./. | ⸬ |

B^bm: ii⌀7   V7   i-

B

E♭ harmonic minor

| E^bm^7 | A^{b7} | $D^b maj^7$ | B^{b7} | |

D^b: ii-7   V7   Imaj7   V7/ii

| E^bm^7 | A^{b7} | $D^b maj^7$ | | ./. |

ii-7   V7   Imaj7

E♭ harmonic minor

| B^{b7} | | ./. | E^bm | | ./. |

E^bm: V7   i-

D.C. al fine

| Gm^{7b5} | C^7 | Fm^{7b5} | B^{b7} | ‖

Fm: ii⌀7   V7 E^bm: ii⌀7   V7

Jazz Study #15: Climb The Stairs

(continued on next page)

Improv Practice

Isolate any new or challenging chord moves in this progression; improvise over 4- and 8-bar chunks and 16-bar sections, targeting chord tones, and using motifs. Find a melodic quote snippet to sneak in somewhere. Start low and slow, build up, then taper off.

Conclusion

The topics in this book take years to learn with consistent practice, so I encourage you to be patient and set up a reasonable routine at a scheduled time every day, and do everything you can to make it enjoyable. You might start with scales and arpeggios, then review a chapter from the book, read/memorize part or all of a new tune, then start a backing track for a tune you know and let it repeat for awhile so you can review its melody and work out some kinks. Keep listening to and transcribing new and challenging music whenever you can. Finally, seek out opportunities to play with and learn from others as much as possible.

Thanks for getting this book and working the program. If you get stuck or have problems with it, use the contact link at monsterguitars.com and I'll get back to you as soon as I can.

Appendix 1: The Fretboard

Traditional neck diagrams like this have the low (thickest) E string at the bottom. In a major scale fingering pattern, the lowest note is not the root. The complete fingering pattern includes all notes of the scale that you can reach without shifting your hand from the area. In Pattern 1, the lowest available scale degree is the 3rd; the highest scale degree is the 5th.

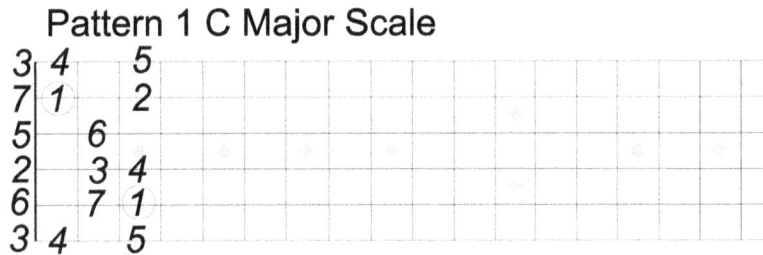

Pattern 1 C Major Scale

```
3 | 4      5
7 | 1      2
5 |    6
2 |    3  4
6 |    7  1
3 | 4      5
```

When first learning a scale, start on a root, play all the available notes in the position, then finish on a root. Each degree (1-7) occurs more than once, so you are repeating the scale in different ranges.

Learning the degree numbers in scale patterns is just as important as learning the names of the notes on the fretboard. Scale degree numbers are used to analyze chords and chord progressions. For example, in a three-note C major chord (a *triad*) there are a root (C), a 3rd (E), and a 5th (G). Mentally turn this vertical frame (usually used for chords) on its left side and compare to the previous one. An X over a string means it is not played.

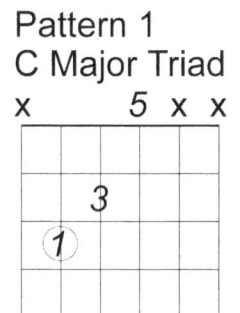

Pattern 1 C Major Triad

```
x        5  x  x
         3
    1
```

Major Scale Formula and Fretboard Patterns

The formula for a scale is created by the locations of the *half steps* (one fret apart when played on the same string) and *whole steps* (two frets apart when played on the same string).

The formula for the major scale is: half steps from 3-4 and 7-8 (8 has the same letter name as 1 but is an *octave* higher). There are whole steps between all the other pitches.

$$1\ 2\ 3\char`^4\ 5\ 6\ 7\char`^8$$

The other way to learn it is to quote the series of whole and half steps.

Whole-Whole-half-Whole-Whole-Whole-half

When played on adjacent strings, a half step is usually a distance of four frets. Here is a half step from the 5th to the 4th string.

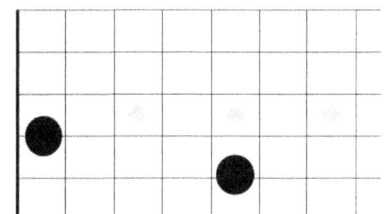

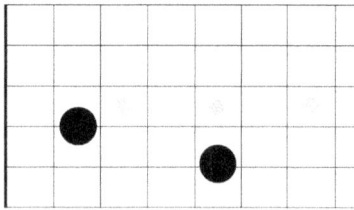

Notes a whole step apart are usually three frets away from each other on adjacent strings. Here is a whole step from string 5 to string 4.

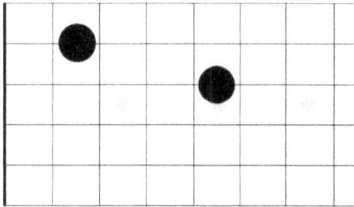

Half steps and whole steps look different between strings 3 and 2 because the tuning interval between those two strings is smaller than between the others. This is a half step from string 3 to string 2.

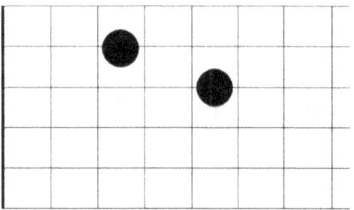

And here's a whole step from string 3 to string 2. Half steps and whole steps underlie all other constructions, so make sure you can play them on one string, or between any two adjacent strings. Include open-string notes. You should learn to name the notes, too, but this can be done a little at a time.

The CAGED System

The major scale patterns have all their half steps (3-4 and 7-8) on one string. This helps you minimize stretches and position shifts while you are playing so it's harder to miss a note.

Pattern 2 C Major Scale

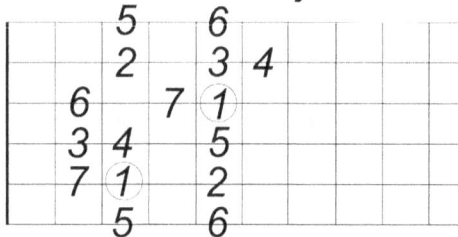

Here is Pattern 2 of the C major scale. For now we're keeping the note C as our root to make it easier see how the five major scale patterns connect to cover the entire fretboard. For this pattern we move up to playing the 5th-string root with the middle finger.

Take your time to visualize Pattern 2, then play it without looking at the diagram. It'll help to recite the whole and half steps of the major scale formula as you play. The roots are on strings 5 and 3, two frets apart. In this pattern, remember to shift the hand position by one fret when crossing between the 3rd and 2nd strings in either direction.

Pattern 1 from the previous page is the first shape (C) of the CAGED sequence, which we can use to find anything we want on the entire fretboard. When played in open position, Pattern 1 gave us the C major scale, the reference for learning chord and scale construction (and other theory) that is common to all instruments.

Why Are These Patterns 1 & 2? I already call this something else!

The CAGED-based 5-pattern system has gradually become the most widely-used, but some teaching methods still use different pattern labeling schemes. If, for example, the previous fingering is called Pattern 4 in the system you learned, that's okay as long as your patterns are numbered consecutively and there are no gaps between patterns on the fretboard.

C, A, G, E, and D are the open-position major chord shapes that when connected end-to-end show the five possible basic fingerings for any chord. Following are the CAGED system major chord shapes (major is implied when the quality is left off the chord name).

C   A   G   E   D

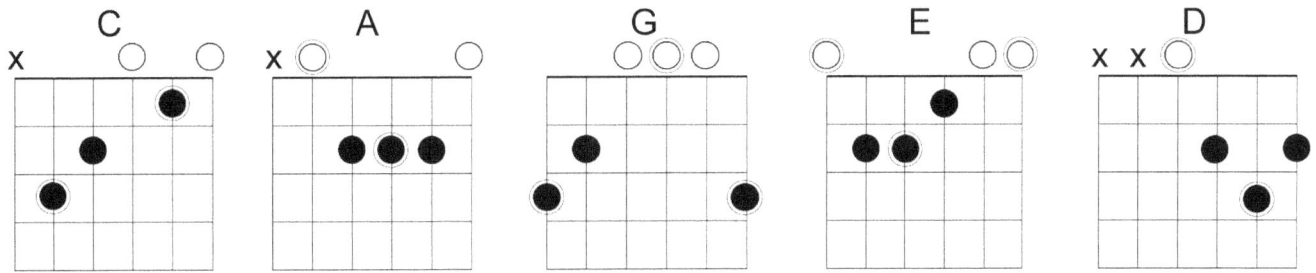

Each of the five shapes produces a C chord when it is played in the proper position to place C notes as its roots. Usually only parts of them are played at one time.

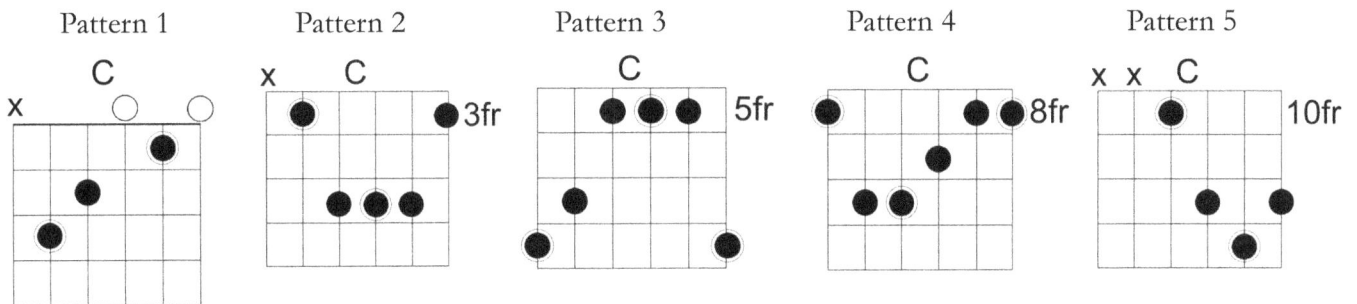

Pattern 1   Pattern 2   Pattern 3   Pattern 4   Pattern 5

C   x C   C   C   x x C
x   3fr   5fr   8fr   10fr

Some of the *root shapes* (they are 1- and 2-octave intervals) in these patterns are also difficult stretches outside of open position, so they do not have to be played; you just need to know where the roots are in relation to one another in each pattern.

Root Shapes in C

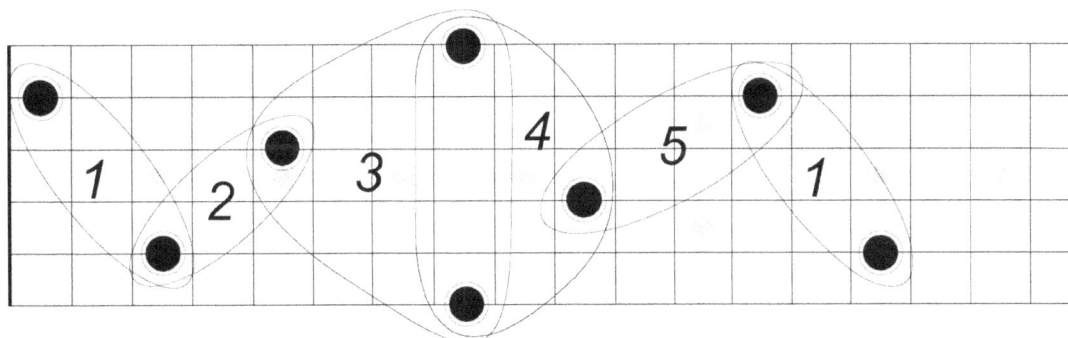

1   2   3   4   5   1

In addition to knowing the scale degree numbers, you'll need to learn the names of the notes on the guitar fretboard so you can understand theory and how melodies fit with chords. Knowing note names is also essential for communication. Make it your goal to learn the location of one note all over the fretboard per week. The five patterns of root shapes in C are a good place to start.

Practice visualizing the root shapes and reciting the locations of the C notes aloud:

1st fret/2nd string   3rd fret/5th string
5th fret/3rd string   8th fret/1st string
8th fret/6th string   10th fret/4th string
13th fret/2nd string   15th fret/5th string
17th fret/3rd string   20th fret/1st string
20th fret/6th string

103

Moving the CAGED Sequence

There is a D note a whole step above each C. Only one of them is shown here.

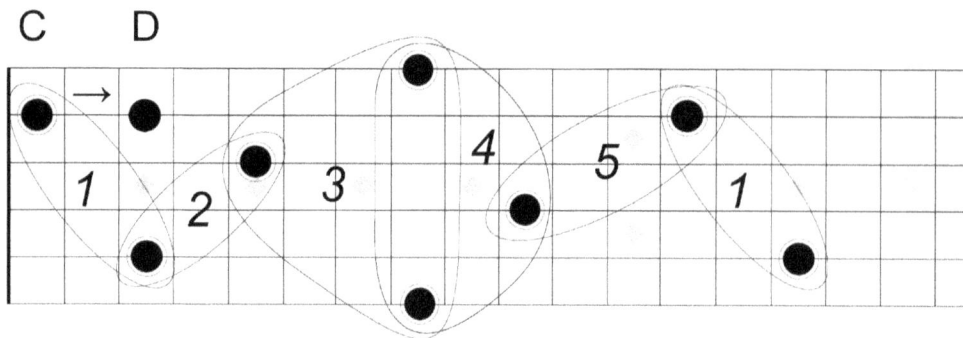

The same five root shapes apply to every D note on the fretboard. The overall CAGED pattern is the same, just two frets higher. The open D string starts a new instance of **Pattern 5**.

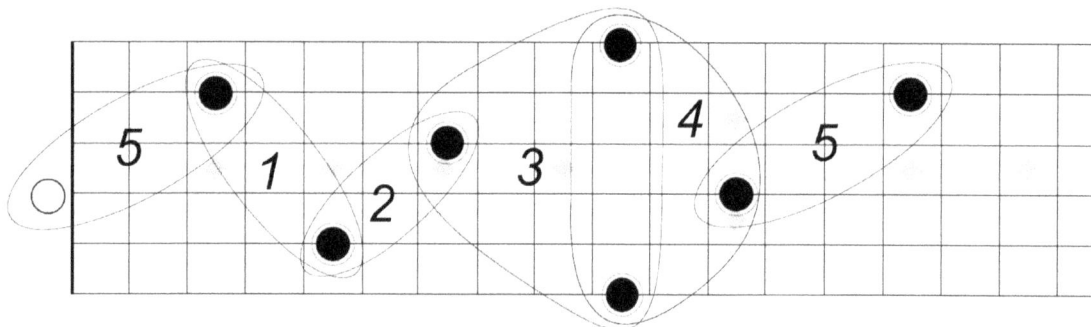

The CAGED system can be used to identify all scale patterns, chord voicings, and melodic shapes. Now on your own, move the system up another two frets to identify the five patterns of E root shapes, and so on.

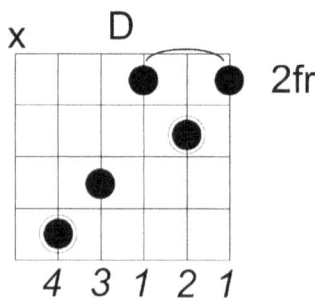

The open C chord shape gives us a D when played at the 2nd fret. The fingering must change; the first finger now barres the two notes that were open strings in the open-position C chord.

Rather than call this chord a "D major chord of the C shape" we'll hereafter refer to everything associated with this root shape as Pattern 1, making this a **Pattern 1 D major chord**. We're still using the CAGED system, but with numbers instead of letters (CAGED=12345), which will simplify the search for the right note or chord in the future.

Pattern 1 D Major Scale

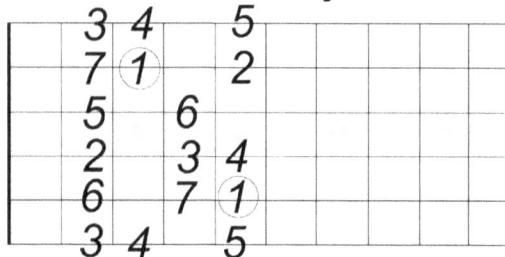

As with the chord, when played away from open position the Pattern 1 major scale is the same shape but uses a different fingering. Now all four fingers are required.

104

Appendix 2: Interval Theory

An interval is the distance between (and including) two notes. The term is also used to refer to those two notes played together as a chord (a *harmonic* interval) or at different times (a *melodic* interval).

An interval gets its correct two-part name by comparison to the major scale. First is the interval number, or *quantity*, which is the same as a major scale degree: 1 through 7, or beyond the octave (8) to as high as needed to describe notes that are farther apart. For example, there's a 15th interval from open E on the 6th string to the open E on the 1st string.

The other part of the interval name is the *quality*. The intervals from the root of a major scale to its degrees are either **major** (2, 3 6, 7) or **perfect** (unison, 4, 5, octave) in quality.

We'll examine quantity and quality with the C major scale first. (It's not the only scale, just the easiest for learning theory stuff.) Here's the C major scale on one string only, making it easy to see that the octave is divided into twelve half steps (one fret each), and that the tones of the major scale are all a whole step apart except for half steps from 3-4 and 7-8.

C Major

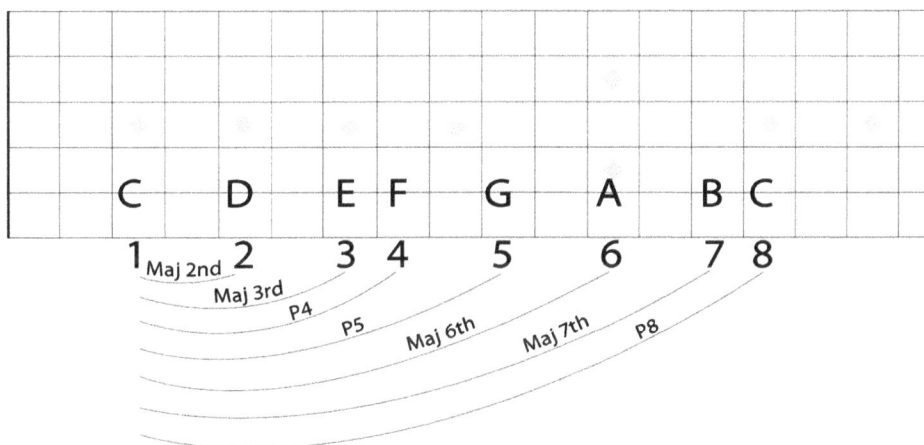

From the root (1) to each tone in the scale defines a reference interval.

1-1 Perfect Unison	= same pitch; zero distance
1-2 Major Second	= 2 half steps or 1 whole step
1-3 Major Third	= 4 half steps or 2 whole steps
1-4 Perfect Fourth	= third plus a half
1-5 Perfect Fifth	= fourth plus a whole
1-6 Major Sixth	= etc.
1-7 Major Seventh	
1-8 Perfect Octave	

It's interesting to note that in music theory there is no concept of "zero." Two notes of the same pitch, while technically having zero pitch difference, are said to be in unison or "as one."

Intervals over a 7th (*compound* intervals) correspond to their references in the lower octave range.

1-8 Perfect Octave (Unison up an Octave)
1-9 Major Ninth (2nd up an Octave)
1-10 Major Tenth (3rd up an Octave)
1-11 Perfect Eleventh (4th up an Octave)
1-12 Perfect Twelfth (5th up an Octave)
1-13 Major Thirteenth (6th up an Octave)
etc.

That's as far up as you need to go to name any chord, although theoretically it goes on ad infinitum.

Minor, Diminished, and Augmented Intervals

The other interval qualities (**minor**, **diminished**, and **augmented**) are created by performing *diminution* or *augmentation* on a major or perfect interval, giving us names covering all possible intervals.

Interval Quality Change Table

	Augmented		
Augment ↑	Major 2, 3, 6, 7	Perfect 1, 4, 5, 8	
	Minor		
Diminish ↓	Diminished		

Looking at the table above we see that diminution of a major 7th by one half step creates a minor 7th. Diminishing the 7th again creates a diminished 7th. Perfect intervals do not have the extra minor possibility and go straight up to augmented or down to diminished in quality.

Look at a major 2nd from C to D. The interval could theoretically be made smaller from either direction:

1) by moving the higher note down. For example, from C to D♭ is a minor 2nd;

OR

2) by moving the lower note UP. From C♯ to D is also a minor 2nd;

but if you are asked to diminish an existing interval or chord, you'd do the first: drop the higher note by the specified amount, so the lower note stays the same.

The same theory applies to making an interval wider. It happens by:

1) moving the higher note up. C to D♯ is an augmented second (and again, to augment an existing interval or chord, this is what you'd do: raise the higher note);

OR

2) moving the lower note down. C♭ to D is also an augmented second.

To those who would proclaim, "Wait a minute. That note is B. There is no such thing as a C♭!" I respond, yes there is. The term for this phenomenon is *enharmonic* spelling. Depending on the situation, it may be correct to call this note C♭, or, for another example, to have an F♯♯ (F×, "F sharp sharp" or "F double-sharp") for the same pitch as G. As a side note, on an instrument that does not adhere to equal-tempered tuning, like a cello, notes like C♭ and B can actually be slightly different-sounding pitches.

Remember the original intervals are all measured from the root of the major scale. If you go between other notes within the scale you will find intervals of various qualities. For example, from 3 to 5 in the major scale is a minor 3rd, because it's a half step plus a whole step.

As with pitches, intervals of the same size in sheer number of half steps can have enharmonic names. For example, a minor 6th is the same distance as an augmented 5th in equal-tempered tuning. How the names are accurately determined is a topic for a book on theory or reading; I'm probably boring you with all this theory business as it is! We do need a bit of it, however, to understand some hands-on soloing concepts in this book.

Hearing the Intervals

Identifying intervals is the first step toward hearing longer melodies, chord qualities, and progressions. Developing your ear will enable you to transcribe the works of others, create better compositions, and improvise solos with more confidence. In an institutional music program students normally advance through many levels of ear training courses. It's a lifelong pursuit.

Start learning to identify the major and perfect intervals first, then add the other qualities at your own pace. It's far more efficient to do this by singing than by playing. Only use your instrument to check your accuracy. First match your voice to a pitch in your vocal range that lets you sing a scale up to the octave. Then slowly sing the steps of a major scale. Only you can determine how hard your exercise should be. Go for the Goldilocks zone: challenging but not discouragingly hard. This approach is good for learning anything new.

When you can sing a major scale, then sing each interval: the tones of a major scale in a melodic pattern that returns to the root after each scale degree. 1-2, 1-3, 1-4, etc.

Intervals in A Major

sing: One Two One   One Three One   One Four One

The tab is for reference. Don't play unless you're stuck.

One Five One   One Six One   One Seven One   One Eight One

Resist the urge to play the notes on your guitar. Only strum the chord or play the notes if you get lost and need to find the tonic (1) again. If you're not sure whether you're getting it, it can help to record yourself and listen (make sure you're singing loud enough) or bring this up in a one-on-one situation with someone you know is qualified to help you.

When you can sing the intervals with some accuracy, then you're ready to identify some that you hear. You can have a friend play intervals and take turns testing each other, make your own recording of a few dozen examples to identify, or look online for a site that creates and tests you on them. I like musictheory.net and tonedear.com. These sites let you customize the test to any level. Just a few minutes each morning, adding pieces and adjusting the difficulty so that your score usually stays in the 90% range, can set your ear up for the rest of the day.

It can be be helpful to reference parts of familiar songs when identifying intervals that you hear. This only works if you can reliably sing the melody you are using, which might take a little practice at first. Depending on your age and background you may prefer to use different mnemonics from the ones on this list.

> Major 2nd - Happy Birthday to You (5-6)*
> Major 3rd - Oh When the Saints Go Marching In
> Perfect 4th - Wedding March (5-8)
> Perfect 5th - Twinkle Twinkle Little Star
> Major 6th - My Bonnie Lies Over the Ocean (5-10)
> Perfect Octave and Major 7th - (Somewhere) Over the Rainbow (1-8-7)

* The songs do not all start from the root of the major scale. For example, the first three notes of "Happy Birthday" go from 5 to 6, which is a major 2nd interval.

When you can accurately sing or hum these melodic bits (or others you may choose), use them for comparison as you identify two-note examples. As you progress, add the minor, and diminished/augmented intervals. Here are more mnemonics.

> Minor 2nd - *Jaws*
> Minor 3rd - Brahms' Lullaby (3-5)
> Augmented 4th/Diminished 5th - *The Simpsons*
> Minor 6th - The Entertainer (3-8)
> Minor 7th - *Star Trek* original closing theme

Once your ear can recognize the basic intervals, stop using the songs and go for direct identification.

Appendix 3: Notation and Key Signatures

You don't need to be a great sight reader to play jazz, but to look at a melody and chord progression and be able play it within an hour rather than a day will be a great help. Reading will help you build a repertoire of standard tunes that you can play, quote from, solo over, and use as a reference for understanding music in general. It's OK to study reading (and ear training, another essential) concurrently with this program. This book does include the training wheels of tablature on most of its examples, but they won't be there in other books you'll need to use. If you're just getting started, find a reading method book specific to guitar (mine is called *Guitar Reading Workbook*).

A chart in a fakebook is usually simpler than the same tune played on a recording. Recorded versions may be embellished and reharmonized so much that they're very hard to copy by ear, especially for a beginner. Learn the basic melody and chords first. The easiest way to start is to read it—but be aware that fakebooks are often mistaken in their transcriptions, so you should also listen carefully to several versions of the song, back to the earliest recordings you can find. As your ear and ability to analyze develop, you can transcribe more difficult music and get information from it that you can knowledgeably put to use, rather than just reciting it.

For now, let's just check out enough notation to get started. At minimum we need to understand the basics like pitch and rhythmic notation, key signatures, and chord symbols, to analyze the music and figure out what to play.

The staff has five lines and four spaces, labeled in alphabetical order from the bottom up. The lines are **E**very **G**ood **B**oy **D**oes **F**ine. The spaces spell **FACE**. Guitar music is written in the treble or "G" clef, the first symbol on the staff. The lower loop surrounds the G note on the second line. Lucky for us, most jazz charts in a "C" book use the same clef.

When notes go below or above the staff, short *ledger lines* are used to continue the alphabet. We'll see one soon.

Most of the examples in this book are in 4/4 time and have primarily eighth-note rhythms. You'll tap your foot four times and count aloud: "1 and 2 and 3 and 4 and" for a total of four beats per measure. The first measure below has eighth notes, which may have flags or be beamed together. You can play this on your open B string. There is an eighth rest (silence) on the "and" of beat 3.

The second measure has a quarter note, which sustains for one beat, forcing the following quarter note to fall on beat 2. A quarter rest on beat 3 puts the next quarter note attack on beat 4. Measure 3 starts with a half rest, forcing whatever follows to fall on beat 3: a half note. Measure 4 has a whole rest. Don't skip any bars like this at the ends of examples; count through them.

Eighth notes are the basic unit in a jazz solo. You may have the urge to play much faster when you hear the examples being demonstrated, but remember, the accompaniment they'll be played over may be at a far higher tempo in real life. When that happens you'll have to change your entire approach rather than just speeding up the eighth notes that you were supposed to learn. Master the eighth note division in 4/4 time. It is your path to success, and also the key to playing faster phrases while maintaining control.

Spelling Scales

Here's one octave of C major scale Pattern 1 written in standard notation and tablature. It's the first scale we study because it follows the **natural half steps** from E-F and from B-C. The natural half steps are not marked on the notation staff but are understood. Because it aligns with the natural half steps, none of the notes need a flat ($\flat$) or sharp ($\sharp$).

Now here's a Pattern 4 F major scale. It follows the formula we've learned, with half steps from 3-4 and 7-8. To make 3-4 a half step we put a flat symbol on degree 4.

Key Signatures

Rather than put a flat on every B throughout a song in the key of F, a key signature is written at the beginning and is understood to always apply unless another change is made. Every B is flat from now on.

To get the next closest key to F (differing from it by only one note), we go up a fourth to B♭. The new key has two flats: B♭ is now the root, and we'll need an E♭ to keep to the major scale formula.

The other flat keys continue in the same order, a fourth higher each time. The flat keys occur in this order:

$$F \; B\flat \; E\flat \; A\flat \; D\flat \; G\flat \; C\flat$$

and the flats that are added to create them follow the same order:

$$B\flat \; E\flat \; A\flat \; D\flat \; G\flat \; C\flat \; F\flat$$

| C major | F major | B♭ major | E♭ major | A♭ major | D♭ major | G♭ major | C♭ major |

Flats: none B♭   B♭ E♭   B♭ E♭ A♭   B♭ E♭ A♭ D♭   B♭ E♭ A♭ D♭ G♭   B♭ E♭ A♭ D♭ G♭ C♭   B♭ E♭ A♭ D♭ G♭ C♭ F♭

Now to the sharp keys. First up, G major shares all the notes in the key of C but needs an F♯ to maintain a half step from 7-8. The corresponding key signature is shown at right.

G A B C D E F♯ G

Each successive sharp key is a 5th higher than the last, making this the order of sharp keys:

$$G \; D \; A \; E \; B \; F\sharp \; C\sharp$$

The sharps themselves are added in this order:

$$F\sharp \; C\sharp \; G\sharp \; D\sharp \; A\sharp \; E\sharp \; B\sharp$$

| C Major | G Major | D Major | A Major | E Major | B Major | F♯ Major | C♯ Major |

Sharps: none F♯   F♯ C♯   F♯ C♯ G♯   F♯ C♯ G♯ D♯   F♯ C♯ G♯ D♯ A♯   F♯ C♯ G♯ D♯ A♯ E♯   F♯ C♯ G♯ D♯ A♯ E♯ B♯

When there is a key change in the music, the new signature may be provided immediately before it. However, in many tunes it is not, because the new key center may be very short, and/or the melody may have been written to stay in the original key while chords from another key are played underneath to add interest. When you solo over these chords, you may need to add tones that were not in the melody. These temporary keys must be interpreted from your knowledge of theory and your trained ears.

Appendix 4: Playing Intervals

There are unlimited possible intervallic playing exercises to expand your fretboard facility. They can be roughly divided into harmonic and melodic studies, though you can of course combine the two for infinite variations.

Harmonic 3rds & 6ths

The first (and easiest) way to start getting harmonic 3rds into your playing is by staying on a set of two strings up and down the neck. These are partial chords, so recite the names as you play them. A two-note chord can also be called a *double stop*.

3rds on every stringset except the 3-2 will use these major and minor shapes. Practice keeping the 1st finger down on the top string as shown here in the ascending portion, and also keeping the 3rd finger down as shown in the descending portion. Usually you'll want a passage like this to have a consistent fingering rather than switching fingers at random.

Harmonic 3rds in C Major

Major and minor 3rds look slightly different on the 3-2 stringset because of the tuning difference.

Harmonic 3rds in B♭ Major

The next most important interval for improvisation is the 6th. 3rds and 6ths are *complementary* intervals, consisting of the same two notes in a different inversion. Notice that these 6ths are exactly the same chords as the 3rds in C on the previous page. You can use 6ths to outline chords, with the top note as the root. Play 6ths without lifting the 2nd finger off the lower string. You'll probably want to use the pick or thumb and a finger (hybrid picking) for string-skipping double stops like this.

Harmonic 6ths in C Major

When 6ths do not cross the 3-2 stringset, the shapes are slightly different. Here they are in B♭ on strings 5 and 3. This time try keeping your 3rd finger down for all the low notes.

Harmonic 6ths in B♭ Major

Playing all the 3rds in a single key with minimal position shifting requires the use of at least two patterns of the CAGED system. Minimizing shifts will allow us to relate the intervals to larger chord shapes and later use them more effectively in progressions. Here we're using Patterns 1 and 2 in D major.

Harmonic 3rds in D Major

The shifting's not necessary for harmonic 6th intervals in position, but they can be tricky because some are on adjacent strings while others require a skip. These will be the same note locations as used in melodic 6ths in Pattern 1.

Harmonic 6ths in D Major

Melodic 3rds & 6ths

When intervals are played melodically (one note at a time) you can stay entirely within a scale pattern. Alternate picking is the way to keep the timing even. Pick down-up (or up-down), over and over, even if it feels weird at first.

Melodic 3rds in B♭ Major Pattern 4

With 6ths you may see an advantage to **outside picking**: a downstroke on the lower string and an upstroke on the higher string in a two-note group. This means you'd start measure 3 with an upstroke.

Melodic 6ths in B♭ Major Pattern 4

To train your fingers to handle any melodic move you can practice all your scales in interval sequences of increasing complexity. This is a good way to warm up your fingers, ears, and brain, instead of playing things you already know. For more on the topic, see *Interval Studies and Lead Guitar Technique*.

Appendix 5: Chords Are Stacks of Intervals

For most of this beginner's book we only use a handful of four-note chord types: maj7, dom7, min7, min7♭5, and the occasional dim7.

Major 7th

The maj7 chord has a root, major 3rd, perfect 5th, and major 7th. It corresponds directly to the major scale. Spelled from C, the notes are C E G B. To get a playable "stock" guitar fingering we rearrange the notes, one per string. There are many ways to do that, but here are the first two to learn. There's a suggested fingering for the Pattern 4 voicing.

Pattern 2
5th-string root
Cmaj⁷

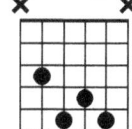

C G B E

Pattern 4
6th-string root
Cmaj⁷

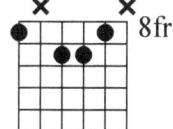

1 3 4 2
C B E G

Be careful to follow the little x marks in these diagrams. The skipped string in the Pattern 4 chord voicing can be tricky. Don't let your first finger collapse onto the unfretted 5th string.

Dominant 7th

The word "dominant" is implied when there is no symbol. There's only a number: 7, 9 , 11, or 13. The 7th chord has a root, major 3rd, perfect 5th, and minor 7th.

Pattern 2
5th-string root
C⁷

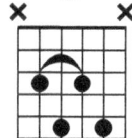

C G E
  B♭

Pattern 4
6th-string root
C⁷

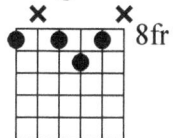

1   2 4 3
C B♭ G
    E

Minor 7th

The minor 7th chord has a root, minor 3rd, perfect 5th, and minor 7th. There is some variation in the way this is written on chord charts: Cm7, C-7, Cmi7, etc. Avoid using an uppercase M—it can be confused for major.

Pattern 2
5th-string root
Cm⁷

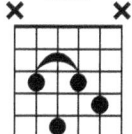

C G E♭
  B♭

Pattern 4
6th-string root
Cm⁷

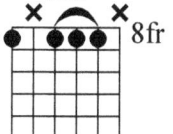

2   3 3 3
C B♭ G
    E♭

117

Minor 7th, Flat 5

Pattern 2
5th-string root
Cm$^{7\flat5}$

1 3 2 4
C G$^\flat$ E$^\flat$
B$^\flat$

Pattern 4
6th-string root
Cm$^{7\flat5}$

2   3 4 1
C B$^\flat$ G$^\flat$
E$^\flat$

The m7$^\flat$5 chord has a root, minor 3rd, diminished 5th, and minor 7th. When heard alone this chord might sound strangely dissonant at first. Dissonance creates tension that will be resolved by an upcoming chord, creating the vital sense that the music is moving. Another symbol for this chord: C$^{\varnothing}$7, per its alternate name, "half-diminished."

Diminished 7th

Pattern 2
5th-string root
Cdim^7

C G$^\flat$ E$^\flat$
B$^{\flat\flat}$

Pattern 4
6th-string root
Cdim^7

2   1 3 1
C B$^{\flat\flat}$ G$^\flat$
E$^\flat$

Here the notes are root, minor 3rd, diminished 5th, and diminished 7th. Sometimes you'll see a little circular symbol (C$^{\circ}$7) instead of "dim."

Cdim^7

Correct enharmonic note names are not always used when verbally describing or writing diminished chords on the staff. (The B$^{\flat\flat}$ in this chord is equivalent to A.) This notation shows the chord in close voicing, then in the two guitar voicings above.

There are some regional variations in how chord symbols are written. For more on the process of building and naming chords and finding useful guitar voicings, check out the *Guitar Fretboard Workbook*.

Here's some practice for stock chords in typical moves. For now we want a single clean strum or pluck on beat 1 or 3 of the measure, with no extra attacks, as each chord rings until it's time for the next one. If these chords are new to you, you may need to move your fingers early in order to find the next shape while staying in steady time. Keep your fingers on or close to the strings, damping any unwanted sounds and minimizing movement. For example, when switching from Fmaj7 to F#dim7 you don't need to move the 3rd and 4th fingers at all. There are other places in these examples where you can keep one or more fingers down as you switch.

Chord Progression Practice

www.ingramcontent.com/pod-product-compliance
Lightning Source LLC
Chambersburg PA
CBHW080519110426
42742CB00017B/3168